AF812577

Contemporary Perspectives On Trauma and Resilience

Floriana Irtelli • Fabio Gabrielli

Contemporary Perspectives On Trauma and Resilience

palgrave
macmillan

Floriana Irtelli
Psychology
Catholic University of the
Sacred Heart
Milano, Italy

Fabio Gabrielli
Philosophy (of the Relationship)
School of Management, Lum
Jean Monnet
Milano, Italy

ISBN 978-3-031-70792-6 ISBN 978-3-031-70793-3 (eBook)
https://doi.org/10.1007/978-3-031-70793-3

© The Editor(s) (if applicable) and The Author(s), under exclusive license to Springer Nature Switzerland AG 2024

This work is subject to copyright. All rights are solely and exclusively licensed by the Publisher, whether the whole or part of the material is concerned, specifically the rights of translation, reprinting, reuse of illustrations, recitation, broadcasting, reproduction on microfilms or in any other physical way, and transmission or information storage and retrieval, electronic adaptation, computer software, or by similar or dissimilar methodology now known or hereafter developed.
The use of general descriptive names, registered names, trademarks, service marks, etc. in this publication does not imply, even in the absence of a specific statement, that such names are exempt from the relevant protective laws and regulations and therefore free for general use.
The publisher, the authors and the editors are safe to assume that the advice and information in this book are believed to be true and accurate at the date of publication. Neither the publisher nor the authors or the editors give a warranty, expressed or implied, with respect to the material contained herein or for any errors or omissions that may have been made. The publisher remains neutral with regard to jurisdictional claims in published maps and institutional affiliations.

This Palgrave Macmillan imprint is published by the registered company Springer Nature Switzerland AG.
The registered company address is: Gewerbestrasse 11, 6330 Cham, Switzerland

If disposing of this product, please recycle the paper.

To Irenaeus Emilius

Contents

Introduction

In the pages of Totalité et Infini from 1961, Emmanuel Lévinas points out how the human, compared to the anonymous flow of the world, makes a gesture of retreat and separation;[1] *the anthropological significance of this gesture, as we shall see, is of absolute magnitude.*

The human is organized from need, the satisfaction of which, that is, enjoyment (the truthfulness of need, the core of his sincerity), allows him, focusing on himself, urging itself, to separate itself from the anonymous and indifferent course of life. Enjoying his needs, man takes a distance from the world; he is happy because he lives. The resulting enjoyment, the enjoyment of enjoyment, the enjoyment of his appetite structure our identity (mine constitutes us as subjects, think of the "this is mine!" of the child), our distancing ourselves from anonymous existence in order to erect ourselves, pose ourselves, define ourselves as other. In other words, the existent poses itself as other than existence by embodying itself on the basis of the logic of my own, the sincerity of my enjoyment, in which, urges E. Lèvinas, saying that I am absolutely for me. Selfish without referring to others—I am alone without loneliness, innocently selfish and alone. At this level, the human is configured as outside all communication, all relationship, deaf to all otherness, metaphorically earless as a hungry belly.

Against the logics of castration, against disembodied, ethereal, worldless spiritualism, E. Lévinas has the enormous merit of claiming full citizenship to an embodied thought. In this way, light, air, and the sincerity of hunger and thirst are restored to people who are properly human.

[1] For further study see the bibliography: E. *Lévinas (1969), Totality and Infinity: An Essay on Exteriority, Alphonso Lingis, transl. Pittsburgh: Duquesne University Press.*

In other words, the happiness of enjoyment.

Compared to Nietzsche, Lévinas addresses, at least on a first level, the logic of life not so much on the basis of appropriation and overpowering over the weak but rather on the ontological level of enjoyment as the foundation of existence, beyond and before any anthropological-moral tracing.

I fulfill my needs, I enjoy, I live, I am happy, nothing more, nothing less.

If enjoyment is an ontological principle, not a faculty or attribute of the subject, the punctum of enfranchisement, by separation from the anonymous flow of the world, which allows us to assert ourselves, holding us steady as beings, the problem arises when the deeply human scene of enjoyment is burst upon by the Other. The other, the otherness, the excess, the beyond of jouissance is configured as a "trauma," a deep laceration of the egotic deafness of enjoyment but also of every rationale, every measure. Compared with animals, the human is not overwhelmed by this traumatic event, that is, the Other, but, through a kind of symbolic web, makes this intrusion the condition, the transcendental, for becoming human, that is, for experiencing.[2] *If we stop at this point in the ontological and anthropological journey, the traumatic encounter with the Other is the human experience of all that is not measurable, governable, categorizable that, nevertheless, we cannot circumvent or avoid since it structures us in relationship, between conflict and recognition, master logics and hospitality, Promethean attempt to measure and acceptance of the other's irrepressible otherness. At a further level, no longer ontological-existential but pathological, as the pages of this book attempt to show, trauma is configured as, at least according to Freud, a deep laceration produced by a particularly intense event to which the subject cannot respond adequately.*

In this sense, especially in an age of such high complexity as ours, in which the same space–time coordinates undergo continuous acceleration and modification, rooted and deep, gestures, postures, styles, forms, figures, and existential contents are subjected to transformations, stresses, and often traumatic declinations.

The pages of this book intend to traverse, in an agile and focused form, the landscapes of trauma between recognition of the fall, fragility, depressive implosions, and possible ways to organize a new universe, anthropological and symbolic, beyond trauma.

[2] For further study see the bibliography Žižek S. (2001) *Die gnadenlose Liebe, Suhrkamp,* Frankfurt am Main.

In particular, we intend to remark on how fragility and its concrete exposure, vulnerability, are constitutive of the human;[3] *thus, how it should be received with extreme care, making care not a mere technical-therapeutic gesture but rather a very human, competent, strenuous attempt to reconstruct in the patient a new and fruitful symbolic universe. All this in the conviction that curing does not mean healing, the prerogative of any God, but rather confronting with competence and empathy the fragile dignity of the suffering person, preserving its uniqueness, vocation, and tension to life.*

Trauma, as one of the manifold experiences of what Karl Jaspers called boundary situations, confirms that the human is fragile and becomes vulnerable, so the main purpose of therapies, beyond schools and orientations, will be to accompany the patient in his or her emotions in his or her experiences of anger, depression, and helplessness to produce new existential traces in which life can flourish again.

[3] Gabrielli F., Irtelli F. (2021) Introductory chapter: "The Transition from Distress to Acceptance of Human Frailty Anthropology and Psychology of the Pandemic Era in Anxiety, Uncertainty, and Resilience During the Pandemic Period—Anthropological and Psychological Perspectives," Intechopen, London.

CHAPTER 1

Reknowing Trauma

Abstract Today when we talk about trauma in the psychological field, we refer to the psychic manifestations of a negative experience that leads to disorganization and dysregulation of a person's biological system. Trauma is thus a psychic reaction, a wound, caused by a traumatic factor (or stressor) that results in an intolerable and distressing emotional impact. Importantly, the capacity to respond to trauma can vary from person to person. According to Ammaniti, trauma represents not only a rupture in everyday experience, but also a split in memory—an event that is often difficult to represent in the mind. This psychological wound may present itself as stunting and amputation of emotions, and its concreteness may persist over time, causing destabilizing mental suffering. We then saw how trauma can have negative effects not only on the psychological level, but also on the biological level, altering the functioning of our organism. Trauma can leave an unprocessed trace that leads us to continually relive the painful event. It was later specified that the reaction to trauma depends on many factors, including the magnitude of the event, the presence or absence of a support figure, the social context and the ability to share the experience. These elements influence the degree of traumatization and the ability to process the trauma. It has also been shown that cognitive processing is a key process in integrating the traumatic memory into our memory and reducing its emotional impact. If processing is hindered by disturbing emotions, the memory remains isolated and easily reactivated by similar stimuli. This can lead to symptoms of anxiety, depression, and

© The Author(s), under exclusive license to Springer Nature Switzerland AG 2024

F. Irtelli, F. Gabrielli, *Contemporary Perspectives on Trauma and Resilience*, https://doi.org/10.1007/978-3-031-70793-3_1

posttraumatic stress. Trauma can provoke a sense of guilt for having suffered the evil, for having allowed it or for having reacted to it; this guilt is often accompanied by shame and self-hatred. This can happen especially if the trauma occurred in childhood; it is described also as the phenomenon that Azieau called "negative attachment" and is based on an attachment to negative, rejecting, or mistreating affective figures. It was then pointed out that trauma is not always determinative of our life trajectory.

Keywords Trauma • Cognitive processing • Traumatic memories • Posttraumatic stress • Anxiety • Distress

Reawareness of Trauma

If only I had known how much harm he was about to do to me, if instead of a vague premonition I could have imagined what deep wound he was about to inflict on me, I certainly would have let out a scream.

Firmly planted on my legs, I would have gone for the essential moan inside me that I was already hearing, pushed it up to my throat, to my mouth, and let it out, at first absurd like foghorns, then shrill like sirens, and finally enormous like a hurricane.

I would have let out a deadly scream and not heard the words that were about to fall on me like so many deadly blades.

M. Cardinal p. 138, 2004[1]

The word "trauma" originates from the Greek and refers to wound, laceration, and damage; in fact, the term is used in somatic medicine to refer to injuries caused by mechanical agents; in neuropsychiatry, on the other hand, this term indicates an injury to the psychic organism as a result of events that break out abruptly in a destructive manner.[2]

In fact, trauma was described by Freud as a kind of "breaking of a protective barrier",[3] that is, it was represented as an unbearable event that can overwhelm human barriers and burst into a person's mind, often leaving him or her overwhelmed. In fact, Freud, with the notion of trauma, refers

[1] For further study, see bibliography: Cardinal M. (2004) Le parole per dirlo, Feltrinelli, Milan, original edition 1975.

[2] For further study, see the bibliography: Amadei G. (2005) Come si ammala la mente, Universale Paperbacks, il Mulino, Bologna.

[3] For further study, see bibliography: Freud F. (1921) Jenseits des Lustprinzips; transl it Beyond the Pleasure Principle, in Works, vol. IX, Turin, Bollati Borighieri, 1986, p. 215.

to "the intensity of an event to which the subject is unable to respond adequately."[4]

Currently, whenever we talk about trauma in the psychological field, we refer to the psychic manifestations of a negative experience from which a disorganization and dysregulation of the person's biological system results. Thus, trauma refers to a physical reaction, a wound caused by a traumatic factor (called a *stressor*) that involves an intolerable and distressing emotional impact.

It is important to specify, in any case, that the capacity to respond to trauma can obviously vary from person to person, as we shall see.

According to Ammaniti,[5] trauma represents not only a rupture in everyday experience but also a split in memory: an event that is often difficult to represent in the mind.

This psychological wound can then present itself as stunting and amputation of emotions, and its concreteness can often persist over time, causing destabilizing mental suffering.

In the early days of the history of psychology, trauma was mainly referred to as war trauma; today, however, we are aware that there are many types of trauma, which may be outside the context of war, and in our days, we are also more informed, for example, of the singular fact that sometimes they may be unconsciously removed and return to consciousness after a long time, unexpectedly, when they are no longer dissociated from memory (i.e., when there are preconditions for becoming conscious of them, *for knowing the trauma again or for reknowing the trauma, as you like*).

To reflect on trauma and its complexity, let us now focus on the stories of two parallel pregnancies: that of Mariastella, a lifelong housewife such as her mother and grandmother, and that of Linda, a career lawyer.

Mariastella could not wait to give birth, and she did not want any anesthetic, as she wanted to feel the full cathartic power of childbirth: she later bragged to her friends about the forty stitches they had given her after giving birth for the lacerations. Her friends commented, "You were so brave." Mariastella is elated about the birth of her son and proclaims to the world how happy she is to be able to exclusively take care of her little

[4] For further study, see bibliography: Freud F. (1915) Triebe und Triebschicksale; tradi t Pulsions and their destinies, in Works, vol. IX, Turin, Bollati Borighieri, 1986 p. 17.

[5] For further study, see bibliography: Ammaniti M. (1999) Those indelible traumas, in "La Repubblica," June 2.

one and how great the pregnancy has been, thanks in part to her mother and grandmother who have always served and revered her. She declares that the pregnancy has truly made her feel reborn and full of energy. Maristella has never been working and was just waiting for this moment to feel fully realized: she exclaims that she will gladly be willing to spend sleepless nights and change little John's diapers: it is a full-time job to do everything expected of a good mom!

On the same day, Linda, a lawyer with a VAT number who had moved to Milan with her partner (also a freelancer) for work-related matters, also gave birth. Linda is an emancipated woman who has always been autonomous, making virtue out of necessity: in fact, her family of origin has always been neglectful and problematic. The pregnancy was not sought by Linda, yet in agreement with her partner, they decided to carry it through despite being without help, unlike Mariastella. When Linda arrived at birth, she was very trying: during pregnancy, in the first few months, the nausea caused by gravidarum turned into copious vomiting, to the point that she was losing weight dangerously. Linda also had an autoimmune disease, which manifested as two relapses during her pregnancy, for which she was rushed to the hospital, and she was immediately informed that doctors would have her aborted if her condition did not improve. She could have risked her life and even lost a child, and the prognosis was declared uncertain. Linda's health fortunately improved, but severe anxiety ensued, which was also worsened by the fact that toward the end of her pregnancy, marked swelling appeared in her hands and feet (edema) that made it difficult for her to walk, wash, and do everything independently. Linda also became covered with large hormonal spots, a fact that she felt was detrimental to her femininity, although transient and marginal compared to all the other issues she had faced. She finally gave birth by emergency C-section because her waters broke earlier than expected, and the baby was in a breech position. The delivery was successful, and when trying to overcome the pain from the operation, Linda reported being plagued by intrusive memories and an unstable mood. Discharged from the hospital, the woman is happy that her baby is healthy, but she asks that she want to start psychotherapy right away because she feels tried and shaken, even though the baby is safe, reports that she continues to have nightmares every night, and daydreams about the dark period when they threatened to have her aborted, and she often has fits of nerves over every matter of daily living. One might ask: is this postpartum depression? Has

Linda experienced pregnancy and related vicissitudes as potentially traumatic experiences?

Each context must be analyzed on its own, and certainly, a brief summary does not do justice to the complexity of the situation.

Upstream, why read these two parallel stories?

It is important to emphasize that different life experiences (such as, for example, pregnancy, which is commonly not considered a traumatic event) may be experienced very dissimilarly by different people: for example, for one woman, motherhood may be the joy of a life, the purpose of an existence; for another person, it may represent an unexpected event, experienced as a potentially traumatic experience because of all the consequences it may entail; in fact, today, we also often speak of "potentially traumatic events,"[6] respecting the individual life trajectories of each human being, his or her experiences, and the specific circumstances he or she encounters; trivially, what for one person may be an occasion of joy, for another may represent a trauma.

Certainly, there are objective and subjective aspects that concur in determining what will or will not become traumatic for an individual, but beyond the variability of the individual person and the share of subjectivity that determines the reaction to an event, when a concrete event and the shock related to it are actually reported in psychotherapy, we cannot help but consider the trauma as a real event that truly happened, even though people may present different reactions: denying a trauma may in fact further traumatize the individual.

Finally, it must be specified that "the idea that traumatic events could lead even normal individuals to illness is far older than the relatively recent creation of the diagnosis of *posttraumatic* stress disorder"[7] in the 1980s, a topic we will address shortly.

[6] For further study, see the bibliography: Irtelli F. (2016) Illuminarsi di Ben-essere, Armando, Rome. pp. 73.

[7] For further study, see the bibliography: Amadei G. (2005) Come si ammala la mente, il Mulino, Bologna. pp. 142.

Various Types of Trauma

As early as 1994, Terr[8] distinguished between traumas of the "first type," that is, those due to a single traumatic experience, and traumas of the "second type," that is, those that take place continuously over time (often under the silence of society and family), which may include, for example, mistreatment, violence, and abuse.

Today, the term *cumulative trauma*[9] has also been coined to describe traumatic situations that continue over time, and there is also talk of a "traumatic atmosphere"[10] to define a daily climate that can harm the person; indeed, Professor Antonello Correale by trauma he does not mean exclusively the single experience capable of bringing about a disruption of the person's cognitive abilities, in a concentrated time but also "in a broader sense the repeated exposure to disturbing or incomprehensible aspects,"[11] especially among people important to the subject.

We must remember, upstream, that there are traumas that, according to the Diagnostic Statistical Manual of Mental Disorders,[12] can cause post-traumatic stress disorder (PTSD)..

What Do We Mean by PTSD?

In 1980, as a result of observations conducted on Vietnam veterans, a new diagnostic category, PTSD, was inserted, which was recognized as a process of adaptation to adverse conditions, and this diagnostic category clarifies how the parade of symptoms depends not only on the vulnerability of the traumatized subject but also on the characteristics peculiar to the event.[13]

[8] For further study see bibliography: Terr L. (1994) Unchained Memories. True Stories of Traumatic Memories, Lost and Found. Basic Books, New York.

[9] For further study, see bibliography: Mucci C. (2014) *Trauma e perdono, una prospettiva intergenerazionale,* Raffaello Cortina Publisher, Milan.

[10] For more details, see bibliography: Mucci C. (2014) *Trauma e perdono, una prospettiva intergenerazionale,* Raffaello Cortina Publisher, Milan.

[11] For further study, see the bibliography: Correale A. (2006) Area traumatica e campo istituzionale, Borla Publisher, Rome p. 135.

[12] For more details, see the bibliography: American Psychiatric Association, DSM-5 Task Force. (2013). Diagnostic and Statistical Manual of Mental Disorders: DSM-5™ (5th ed.). American Psychiatric Publishing, Inc, Washington DC, it. Trad. (2014) Raffaello Cortina Editore, Milan.

[13] For further study, see the bibliography: Amadei G. (2005) Come si ammala la mente, Universale Paperbacks, il Mulino, Bologna.

For a diagnosis of PTSD to occur, it is necessary for the subject (regardless of his or her characteristics) to experience an event in which death, the threat of death, or serious injury or threat to one's own or others' physical integrity is involved.

A person's response in that situation typically includes intense fear, feelings of helplessness or horror.

More specifically, how does posttraumatic stress disorder manifest itself?[14]

To make a diagnosis of PTSD, some of these symptoms must be present for more than one month for each category listed here:

- **Intrusive symptoms**[15] include involuntary unpleasant memories, trauma-related unpleasant dreams, dissociative reactions such as flashbacks,[16] psychological distress, and physiological relations in the face of trauma-related stimuli.
- **Symptoms related to avoidance of trauma-related stimuli**[17] include avoidance or attempt to avoid unpleasant memories and thoughts related to the trauma and avoidance or attempt to avoid external factors (people, things, places, situations) that arouse unpleasant memories related to the trauma.

[14] For more details, see the bibliography: American Psychiatric Association, DSM-5 Task Force. (2013). Diagnostic and Statistical Manual of Mental Disorders: DSM-5™ (5th ed.). American Psychiatric Publishing, Inc, Washington DC, it. Trad. (2014) Raffaello Cortina Editore, Milan. p. 314–315.

[15] One or more symptoms in this category. For more details, see the bibliography: American Psychiatric Association, DSM-5 Task Force. (2013). Diagnostic and Statistical Manual of Mental Disorders: DSM-5™ (5th ed.). American Psychiatric Publishing, Inc, Washington DC, it. Trad. (2014) Raffaello Cortina Editore, Milan. pp. 314–315.

[16] The subject feels or acts as if the traumatic event is recurring by experiencing intrusive and repetitive memories. For further discussion see bibliography: American Psychiatric Association, DSM-5 Task Force. (2013). Diagnostic and Statistical Manual of Mental Disorders: DSM-5™ (5th ed.). American Psychiatric Publishing, Inc, Washington DC, it. Trad. (2014) Raffaello Cortina Editore, Milan. n p. 314–315.

[17] One or two criteria of the two listed in this category must be present. For more details, see the bibliography: American Psychiatric Association, DSM-5 Task Force. (2013). Diagnostic and Statistical Manual of Mental Disorders: DSM-5™ (5th ed.). American Psychiatric Publishing, Inc, Washington DC, it. Trad. (2014) Raffaello Cortina Editore, Milan. pp. 314–315.

- **The following negative alterations in thoughts and emotions are associated with the trauma:**[18] inability to recall some important aspect of the trauma, persistent and exaggerated negative beliefs or expectations about oneself and the world and/or about the cause and/or consequences of the trauma, persistent negative emotional state, marked reduction in interest or participation in meaningful activities, feelings of detachment and/or estrangement from others, and persistent inability to experience positive emotions.
- **Altered arousal**[19] **and excessive reactivity to any trauma-related stimulus:**[20] irritable behavior and/or anger outbursts, reckless and/or self-destructive behavior, hypervigilance, exaggerated alarm responses, concentration problems, and sleep-related difficulties.

PTS is associated with a variety of symptoms, and one of the curious aspects concerns precisely the paradoxical nature of trauma-related memories, which can be very vague or, conversely, intrusive and very vivid;[21] symptoms, in fact, include functions such as memory and the difficulty of integrating memories into memories involved.

It should be emphasized that not only memory can be affected by trauma but also social relationships: often individuals characterized by PTSD become susceptible and explode in angry outbursts, experiencing tension for trivial reasons, even in the presence of those closest to them. Indeed, both increased reactivity to stimuli and an inability to manage one's emotions may occur overall; in short, the impact of trauma can tangentially have significant consequences on interpersonal relationships as well.

[18] Two or more criteria from this group of symptoms in this category must be present. For more details, see the bibliography: American Psychiatric Association, DSM-5 Task Force. (2013). Diagnostic and Statistical Manual of Mental Disorders: DSM-5™ (5th ed.). American Psychiatric Publishing, Inc, Washington DC, it. Trad. (2014) Raffaello Cortina Editore, Milan. n p. 314–315.

[19] That is, the intensity of psychophysiological activation of an organism.

[20] Two or more of the criteria listed in this category must be present. For more details, see the bibliography: American Psychiatric Association, DSM-5 Task Force (2013). Diagnostic and Statistical Manual of Mental Disorders: DSM-5™ (5th ed.). American Psychiatric Publishing, Inc, Washington DC, it. Trad. (2014) Raffaello Cortina Editore, Milan. p. 314–315.

[21] For further discussion, see bibliography: Williams R. ed. (2009) Trauma e relazioni, le prospettive scientifiche e cliniche contemporenee, Raffaello Cortina Publisher, Milan.

The effects of trauma can also affect the individual's self: often when PTSD develops, loss of self-esteem occurs, a topic we will explore in the next section.[22]

We must also specify at this point that the diagnosis of PTSD is still not sufficient to grasp the complexity of suffering related to trauma because, on the one hand, even those who do not develop PTSD can suffer a great deal and experience, for example, deep depression, and on the other hand, not all people exposed to a so-called traumatic event, whatever it may be, come to develop a severe reaction. Each individual situation must be evaluated on its own.

It is then fair to point out that there is no direct relationship between the bravery an individual may have and whether he or she suffers from PTSD; for example, in World War I, men who had developed shell shock were decorated to the same extent as other soldiers, and among the decorated people, there is an abundance of officers suffering from PTSD;[23] each situation is unique.

If, purely for the sake of brevity, the traumas that can give rise to PTSD can be called metaphorically Trauma with a *capital T*, the traumas that *cannot* give rise to PTSD can be called *trauma with a lower case t* (e.g., abandonment, rejection, neglect, and mistreatment). It must be specified that this last type of trauma, although it does not directly expose one to the risk of death, can still cause serious distress to the subject: events may take place, for example, that can be repeated many times, which may also distort one's sense of the world and sense of self, for example, a parent's repeated expression of contempt toward a child may lead the child to think that he or she is defective,[24] or an individual may be a victim of racism because he or she is a member of a social minority, and again, these are repeated events, such as microaggressions, which generally do not

[22] For further study, see the bibliography: Amadei G. (2005) Come si ammala la mente, Universale Paperbacks, il Mulino, Bologna.

[23] For further study, see bibliography: Miller E. (1940) Neuroses in War. Macmillan, London.

[24] In these cases, dysfunction emerges from chronic repeated experiences and processes, mainly interpersonal relational experiences and somatic and brain processes For further discussion, see the bibliography: Tronick E. (2022) Trauma never occurs only once: being traumatized by a slap is like making meaning of the game of peek-a-boo, Psychoanalytic dialogs, 2022, Vol 32, N, 6, 661 673.

endanger the person's life but can still have a serious negative impact on the person's mental health.[25]

Combining the categories now presented regarding trauma, we can in summary state that there can be Traumas with a *capital T* and *Traumas with a lower case t* that can occur only once in a lifetime, thus falling under Terr[26] category of the "first type," or they can occur over and over again, falling under Terr category of the "second type," and the latter traumas can thus also be called *cumulative traumas.*

Beyond the categories just mentioned, Gherardo Amadei specified that in determining the onset of a severe reaction to a trauma, one must consider upstream "the magnitude of the event,"[27] which in some cases can be extreme; let us take an example in this regard: Edith Eva Eger was deported to Auschwitz. On the very day of her arrival, her parents were killed; on the other hand, she was asked to dance in public for the Nazis, humiliating her. It was the first in a series of tortures, which lasted a very long time. This was her fate and that of many other SS prisoners who also lived daily under threat of death.

Clearly, this is a type of trauma that has a very high probability of causing PTSD and falls into the category of the "second type," but not only that, in this regard, it is possible to point out that among the various types of trauma we can also speak of "massive social trauma,"[28] which refers to devastating experiences such as exterminations, cleansing in ethnicity, genocides, wars; in these cases, there is a collectivity that organizes itself to harm both the individual and the entire social and/or cultural group of which this individual is a part.

In such situations, traumatic experiences are obviously linked to borderline situations, such as loss of family members, loss of bodily integrity, loss of protection of kin support, loss of home, living with traumatized people, separation of family members, and loss of schooling opportunities.

[25] For further discussion, see bibliography:Tummala-Narra P. (2023) Awakening to racial trauma faced by Asian Americans, Psychoanalytic dialogs, 2023, Vol, 33, No. 1, 77–86.

[26] For further study see bibliography: Terr L. (1994) Unchained Memories. True Stories of Traumatic Memories, Lost and Found. Basic Books, New York.

[27] For further study, see the bibliography: Amadei G. (2005) Come si ammala la mente, Universale Paperbacks, il Mulino, Bologna. p. 150.

[28] For further study, see bibliography: Mucci C. (2014) *Trauma e perdono, una prospettiva intergenerazionale,* Raffaello Cortina Publisher, Milan p. 62.

The magnitude of the trauma is objectively extreme in such cases, even though individual reactions may be very different from each other.[29] It should be emphasized again that every reaction to trauma is subjective, but objectively, situations such as the ones described above are extreme conditions, and it should be specified in this regard that, in such circumstances, although each individual may present a reaction of his or her own, allowing oneself to define trauma as "relative" is neither rational nor appropriate.

Upstream, to understand each individual's reaction to trauma, regardless of its category of reference, one must certainly consider how each individual copes with trauma, including in terms of how he or she usually tends to manage his or her emotions; in fact, it should be added that in this regard, past and present individual psychopathology also has a certain bearing, and it is important to assess as well the person's life history and past experiences, as well as current life contingencies: being in a period of life that can already be defined as critical, that is, one that has already tested the individual's safety base and adaptive capacity, upstream argues in favor of the onset of a severe reaction to trauma. Thus, the characteristics of the person interact with the type of trauma and

> *It follows from these considerations that exceptionally strong events (with high magnitude) can almost inevitably produce psychopathological disorders independently of subjective variables, while seemingly trivial events can produce disorders in the presence of strongly disadvantageous subjective variables.*
> *Amadei, 2005, p. 150*[30]

Finally, the early age of the potentially traumatized person may also be relevant to the development of trauma. In this regard, we can emphasize that one must consider with particular attention precisely the age and developmental stage of the person: the younger his or her age is, the more significant the impairments might be once he or she becomes an adult. Having experienced childhood trauma generally increases people's vulnerability.[31]

[29] For further study, see the bibliography: Amadei G. (2005) Come si ammala la mente, Universale Paperbacks, il Mulino, Bologna.

[30] For further study, see the bibliography: Amadei G. (2005) Come si ammala la mente, Universale Paperbacks, il Mulino, Bologna.

[31] For more details, see bibliography: Amadei G. (2005) Come si ammala la mente, Universale Paperbacks, il Mulino, Bologna.

Traces of Trauma

The need to defend oneself does not end when the trauma is concluded because a residue of something unprocessed remains.

Bromberg P.M., 2011, p. 49[32]

There is now a large and sufficiently established literature confirming that in the presence of certain traumatic situations, especially extreme ones repeated over time (such as the state of war and sexual abuse between family members), neurophysiological and biochemical alterations can be detected.

Amadei G., 2005, p. 150[33]

Trauma can impair not only the sense of self-integrity and emotional, cognitive, affective, and relational functioning as anticipated but also the biological functioning of the individual.

Unusual pain sensitivity or exceptionally high pain tolerance, stress-related headaches, frequent blinking or failure to keep eyelids open, narcoleptic symptoms, and physical symptoms without a diagnosable medical cause can often be related to trauma.

Fisher J. 2017, p. 39[34]

As explained by Gherardo Amadei,[35] the individual's reaction to traumatic events of various kinds is a product of the subjective response to the events, which could coincide with the development of a disorder, but it could also belong to the spectrum of normality. In fact, as already anticipated, many factors intervene in determining how traumatic an event is: the traces of trauma concern both the combination of the abovementioned "magnitude of the event" and a set of subjective, interpersonal, and social variables.

The importance of the "magnitude of the event" factor in the development of PTSD symptomatology is intuitive: the greater the magnitude of

[32] For further discussion, see the bibliography: Bromberg P. M. (2011) The shadow of the tsunami. The growth of the relational mind. Tr. it. Raffaello Cortina, Milan, 2012.

[33] For further study, see the bibliography:Amadei G. (2005) Come si ammala la mente, Universale Paperbacks, il Mulino, Bologna.

[34] For further discussion, see bibliography: Fisher J. (2017). Guarire la frammentazione del sé. Come integrare le parti del sé dissociate dal trauma psicologico. Raffaello Cortina Publisher, Milan.

[35] For further study, see the bibliography: Amadei G. (2005) Come si ammala la mente, Universale Paperbacks, il Mulino, Bologna.

the trauma, the greater may be the difficulty encountered by the subject; on the other hand, the factors involved in defining the level of traumatization are also the presence or absence of a reference figure as a source of consolation. In fact, it can also have a strong influence on the course of the trauma to have or not have support from loved ones and/or an extended circle of people: in the development of trauma, the importance of the social context is significant.

> *Presumably, an experience becomes traumatic,* i.e., *injurious to the integrity-continuity of the essential functions of the apparatus, not only and not so much because of the presence of fear and pain factors but also because of the simultaneous absence of the social relations that by innate means (...) are expected to intervene to offer protection or at least mitigate pain.*
> *Liotti G., 2005, p. 132*[36]

In this regard, Amadei[37] pointed out that when there is *no* social sharing of the trauma, there may be a trace of it through the phenomenon of *mental rumination* that can take the place of processing: thinking about the traumatic event becomes a kind of endless mental reiteration, which prevents the achievement of emotional balance.

It is precisely the disruption of cognitive processing of information that can produce disturbing memories that are not processed (and this can happen for both trauma with a *capital T* and *trauma with a lower case t*), so it is important to facilitate the processing of disturbing material in psychotherapy so that the past memory is not continually re-experienced and reactivated in the present but can be dealt with in a more evolved and detached way.

Disruption of memory processing can be caused by high levels of disturbed emotions. If processing does *not* occur, the information remains enclosed in a neural network in its original state and is stimulated by various stimuli that resemble the initial memory, not infrequently causing flashbacks and unpleasant emotions.[38]

[36] For further discussion, see the bibliography: Liotti G. (2005) Trauma and dissociation in the light of attachment theory. In Childhood and adolescence, 4, 3, pp. 130–144.

[37] For further study, see the bibliography: Amadei G. (2005) Come si ammala la mente, Universale Paperbacks, il Mulino, Bologna.

[38] For more details, see the bibliography: Spanocchi P. (2001), Cenerini M., *Stress, trauma e psicoterapia nella emergenza quotidiana*. Medicea, Florence.

This factor can generalize over time and be the basis for the development of anxiety, depression, and posttraumatic stress.[39]

How can other significant traces of the trauma remain?

In terms of overpowering emotions and intrusive images, because all images, sounds, and sensations related to the original moment mentally remain in the same state in which they were experienced, as they were not processed, some are constantly re-experienced at the psychological level; in fact, when perceptions of the present connect to mnemonic networks, various components of previously unprocessed memories (emotions, physical sensations, thoughts/conceptions) are re-experienced.

Shocking memories are also often partly dissociated from the subject's general affective and semantic network and may be represented in a form that leads to distortions in perceptions, feelings, and responses.[40]

In summary, trauma can involve interference in the processing of memories and emotions, and all these occurrences not infrequently can also generate in people irrational beliefs and deadening conceptions about themselves and reality related to a nonprocessing of the event.

All of these factors may represent experiences that contribute to the subject's malaise: as a result of experiencing sudden and uncontrollable events, which the subject has experienced in a traumatic way, he or she may develop a generic expectation of danger and uncontrollability of the surrounding reality, and a conception of self as powerless and incapable, a lowering of self-esteem may then take place, as anticipated.

It can also come down to the subjective perception of any stimulus as dangerous, which results not only in the subject avoiding certain situations but also in posttraumatic symptomatology lasting over time.

The development of "learned helplessness," a concept studied by Seligman,[41] can be added to this research.

This scholar has shown that the experience of repeatedly feeling overwhelmed, defeated, paralyzed, and vulnerable can easily affect the subject, who may develop a constant sense of helplessness.

[39] For more details, see bibliography: previous note.

[40] For further study, see the bibliography: Edna B. Foa, Keane T.M., Friedman M. (2000) (eds.) *Effective treatments for PTSD: practice guidelines from the International Society for Traumatic Stress Studies*, Guilford press, New York London.

[41] For further study, see bibliography:Seligman, M.E.P. (1977), Helplessness: On Depression, development and death, Freeman, San Francisco.

If forms of helplessness are prolonged over time, individuals may develop a constant resigned attitude toward life and experience difficult situations.

A sense of pessimism and hopelessness can thus take root, which can take a toll on the mood of those who develop learned helplessness and expose them to a serious risk of depression, thus losing the ability to react and purpose: we suffer most when we think we cannot influence the course of events and are convinced that our actions cannot in any way improve our lives.

In summary, it may take only a few episodes in which the person has felt defeated, is vulnerable, and has no way to produce learned helplessness, which can render the person incapable of responding.

"So Monstrous That I Do Not Remember It": Dissociation

What are you doing? He asked, but his father did not answer, and Patrick was too frightened to repeat the question. His father's hand held him pressed against the bed; his face wedged between the folds of the bedspread, Patrick could hardly breathe. He stared at the curtain rod above the open window. He could not understand what form the punishment was taking, but he knew his father must be very angry with him to hurt him so much. He could not bear the sense of helplessness that had overwhelmed him. He could not bear the injustice he had suffered. He did not know who the man was: it could not be his father who had annihilated him so ruthlessly. From the curtain rod, if he could have reached him, he could have watched the whole scene from the comfort of his seat, just as his father watched him, from above. For a moment, Patrick had the feeling of being up there and witnessing with detachment the punishment inflicted by a stranger on a child. He tried with all his might to focus again on the curtain rod, and this time, the feeling lasted longer: he was sitting there, his arms folded, and he was leaning against the wall. Back on the bed, with a strange sense of emptiness, bearing the weight of not knowing what was going on. He could hear his father gasping and the bed keyboard banging against the wall. From behind the green bird curtain, he saw a gecko peeping out, standing, motionless, at the corner between the two walls, next to the open window. Patrick reached out toward the lizard, clenching his fists until his own concentration turned into a telephone wire stretched between them. Patrick vanished behind the gecko's skin. The gecko must have understood because at that very instant, it slithered out the window and along the outer wall of the mansion.

St. Aubyn, 1992, p. 81[42]

It cannot be true that all this happened to me; otherwise, someone would have come to help.

Ferenczi S., 1932, P. 76[43]

As already anticipated, trauma can change a person's brain structure and function,[44] and individuals under severe stress can also cause play dissociation, as described in the first example by St. Aubyn: this is "an autohypnotic process that anesthetizes and isolates pain."[45]

In this regard, the specificity of the trauma can have unique consequences; for example, those who experience violence in childhood are more likely to suffer from dissociative symptoms and amnesia, so it has been considered that violence experienced in childhood has different consequences than, for example, that of a cataclysm or other circumscribed trauma in adult life.[46] It has also been shown that those who dissociate at the time of trauma are more vulnerable to posttraumatic reactions.[47]

As Bromgerg states, dissociation enters the field when "a chaotic flow of unadjustable affects in the mind takes place, threatening the stability of the self and sometimes mental health itself."[48]

Dissociation, in short, is a reaction to trauma because it represents an attempt to survive what consciousness cannot bear.

To survive, the traumatized person may dissociate; therefore, in these cases, the first phase of psychotherapy is often devoted to building a therapeutic and trusting alliance and then later comes to deal with traumatic memories, which may also be dissociated.

[42] For further study, see bibliography: St. Aubyn E. (1992) The Melrose. Tr. it. Neri Pozza, Vicenza 2012.

[43] For further study, see bibliography: Ferenczi S. (1932) Clinical Diary. January–October 1932. Raffaello Cortina, Milan 1988.

[44] For further study, see bibliography: Mucci C. (2014) *Trauma e perdono, una prospettiva intergenerazionale,* Raffaello Cortina Publisher, Milan.

[45] For further discussion, see bibliography: Schwaryz H.L. (1994) From dissociation to negotiation: a relational psychoanalytic perspective on multiple personality disorder. In Psychoanalytic Psychology, 11, p. 189–231. p. 191.

[46] For further discussion, see bibliography: Williams R. ed. (2009) Trauma e relazioni, le prospettive scientifiche e cliniche contemporenee, Raffaello Cortina Publisher, Milan.

[47] For more details, see bibliography: previous note.

[48] For further study, see the bibliography: Bromberg P. M. (2011) The shadow of the tsunami. The growth of the relational mind. Tr. it. Raffaello Cortina, Milan, 2012 p. 49.

It is crucial to specify again that not giving proper attention to what is real, or what may have happened that is real, risks retraumatizing the person, even during psychotherapy, precisely if the repetition of the denial of reality by an adult who represents an authority happens, because usually in the past, there was another adult who had a duty to be a witness to the trauma and instead preferred to pretend not to see.

The psychotherapeutic path, on the contrary, leads to reknowing the trauma to face and process it even if it seems to be an event suspended in time.[49]

> *Devoid of a chronological record of what happened but vulnerable to the unsolicited activation of trauma-related bodily sensations and memories, individuals inherit a range of symptoms and reactions without a framework to identify them as memories. Later, trauma survivors present to therapy describing their distress, depression, shame, low self-esteem, loneliness and alienation, problems with anger, and impulsivity (.). They may be plagued by chronic expectations of danger: anxiety and then intrusive fears, hypervigilance ("I have eyes in the back of my head"), chronic shame and self-loathing, the belief that the worst is about to happen, helplessness and hopelessness, fear of abandonment, dulling and disconnection from emotions.*
>
> *Fisher J. 2017 p. 28–29*[50]

Attachment to the Negative

After trauma, one may develop not only low self-esteem, depression, and a sense of helplessness but also guilt, "attachment to the negative,"[51] "death instinct,"[52] and "traumatic attachments."[53]

[49] For further discussion, see bibliography: Lingiardi V. Preface in Mucci C. (2014) Trauma e perdono, una prospettiva psicoanalitica intergenerazionale, Raffaello Cortina Publisher, Milan.

[50] For further discussion, see the bibliography: Fisher J. (2017). Guarire la frammentazione del sé. Come integrare le parti del sé dissociate dal trauma psicologico. Raffaello Cortina Publisher, Milan.

[51] For further discussion, see the bibliography: Anzieu D. (2012) Créer-Détruire: Le travail psychique créateur, Dunod, Paris, p. 103.

[52] For further study, see bibliography: Mucci C. (2014) *Trauma e perdono, una prospettiva intergenerazionale,* Raffaello Cortina Publisher, Milan p. 54. For further study, see bibliography: also Lingiardi V. Preface in Mucci C. (2014) Trauma e perdono, una prospettiva psicoanalitica intergenerazionale, Raffaello Cortina Publisher, Milan, p. IX.

[53] For further study, see bibliography: Albasi C. (2012) Attaccamenti traumatici: modeli operativi interni dissociati, UTET, Turin University, Turin; Albasi C. (2012) Dissociated Internal Working Models: A relational perspective on attachment, trauma and dissociation, Nova Science Publishers Inc, New York. For further discussion, see bibliography: also Irtelli F. (2021) Sul perdono, l'esperienza umana della rinascita, La Bussola Publisher, Rome.

In fact, it may paradoxically happen that the traumatized individual even feels guilty for having suffered the trauma, and the guilt the individual feels is not infrequently accompanied by shame for his own weakness and self-hatred for having allowed someone to hurt him.[54]

> *It is possible not to forgive ourselves for "allowing" someone to hurt us because the wrong perpetrator has revealed to our eyes how vulnerable and fragile we are.*
> *Barcaccia B., 2013, p. 197*[55]

It is also worth mentioning that:

> *The presence of abuse, particularly sexual abuse, in childhood has a strong correlation with difficulty in forgiving oneself in adulthood.*
> *Barcaccia B., 2013, p. 208*[56]

It is also interesting to note that this form of self-blame is often present and may prove resistant to change in cases where the trauma occurred at a very early age; for example, patients tend to feel guilty for not having done enough to stop the mistreatment even though they were 5–6 years old when they were victimized, and therefore, unlike an adult, they did not have the tools to resist it.

Unfortunately, these individuals typically feel that they are guilty as well of their own reactions to the trauma and of the feeling of shame with respect to their past history.[57]

It often happens that when an individual has been victimized by someone or something, a part of his or her mind also identifies with the perpetrator, and sometimes the person adopts the attitude of the perpetrator toward himself or herself, denying himself or herself the chance to be well, for example, actively seeking new situations that are a source of discomfort and new trauma.

[54] For further study, see bibliography: Irtelli F. (2021) Sul perdono, l'esperienza umana della rinascita, La Bussola Publisher, Rome.

[55] For further study, see the bibliography: Barcaccia B., Mancini F. (2013) Teoria e clinica del perdono, Raffaello Cortina, Milan.

[56] For more details, see bibliography:previous note.

[57] For further study, see bibliography:Irtelli F. (2021) Sul perdono, l'esperienza umana della rinascita, La Bussola Publisher, Rome.

In this regard, we can now reflect on both the "negative attachment" theme described by Anzieu[58] and the "death drive" theme described by Lingiardi and Mucci[59] (in a very different way from how Freud originally understood it) and the "traumatic attachments" described by Albasi.[60]

Anzieu explains that "attachment to the negative"[61] is an expression that refers to the fact that the child, and later the adult, may become attached to a negative, that is, rejecting or abusive (thus potentially traumatizing) maternal image.

We may ask why a person who has been abused by his or her mother often continues to choose situations in adult life that resemble the original situation. Why does a person tend to love people who have hurt him or her and will hurt him or her?

Negative attachment combines a negative experience of attachment to a discouraging parental figure with a fixation on attachment even in adulthood to reference figures who respond negatively to repeated requests for tenderness.

According to Anzieu, this kind of past is not uncommon in abused children and battered women, who often remain in the same situation they experienced in childhood, remaining attached to, for example, their abusive partner and/or the abusive parents themselves.[62]

Therefore, one may ask why is it that in certain cases, the child grows up and, as an adult, remains attached to rejecting and/or abusive figures? Why does he continue in his life to love the people who hurt him?

In summary, negative attachment is also manifested by a fixation of attachment to love objects that respond negatively to repeated requests for

[58] For further discussion, see the bibliography:Anzieu D. (2012) Créer-Détruire: Le travail psychique créateur, Dunod, Paris. p. 103.

[59] For further study, see bibliography: Lingiardi V. Preface in Mucci C. (2014) Trauma e perdono, una prospettiva psicoanalitica intergenerazionale, Raffaello Cortina Publisher, Milan; for further study see bibliography se also Mucci C. (2014) *Trauma e perdono, una prospettiva intergenerazionale,* Raffaello Cortina Publisher, Milan.

[60] For further discussion, see bibliography: Albasi C. (2012) Dissociated Internal Working Models: A relational perspective on attachment, trauma and dissociation, Nova Science Publishers Inc, New York.

[61] For further discussion, see the bibliography: Anzieu D. (2012) Créer-Détruire: Le travail psychique créateur, Dunod, Paris. p. 103.

[62] For more details, see bibliography: previous note.

affection,[63] to potentially traumatic figures, which are sought out because they appear in any case upstream familiar and therefore already known.

Lingiardi and Mucci also describe the "death drive" in this regard and state that it, as it can be understood today, has an interpersonal characteristic, and we can see it in action in addiction to traumatizing relationships and encounters.[64]

> Mucci states that this dynamic "*is learned from the environment and is the result of environmental relationships that, instead of being life-giving, become death-bringing.*"
>
> *Mucci C. 2014 p. 54*[65]

A vicious circle may thus develop, either on the basis of "an attachment to the negative" or on the basis of "a death drive." We therefore also specify that the so-called victim may then, in turn, probably play an active role in seeking out potentially traumatizing situations again: it is not uncommon for the victim to place himself or herself back into an abusive relationship because he or she may also have low self-esteem.

Deadly relational entanglements can then be created, in which, for example, the abuser can reinforce his control over his neighbor by continuing to belittle and attack him (thus confirming what the sufferer thinks, regardless, about himself).

The attacker may then try to strengthen the bond with the other by convincing him that no one accepts him and no one wants him: maintaining the low self-esteem of the one underneath helps the oppressor to exert his control and confirms to the one underneath the idea of his own devalued image, paradoxically giving him reason in his own implicit beliefs (this may, for example, confirm the attacks that parents used to field during childhood and adolescence, thus proposing a situation that "feels familiar" to the subject and is therefore unconsciously accepted).[66]

[63] For more details, see bibliography: previous note.

[64] For further study, see the bibliography: Liotti G. (2005) The interpersonal dimension of consciousness, Carocci publisher, Rome p. 231.

[65] For further discussion, see bibliography: Lingiardi V. Preface in Mucci C. (2014) Trauma e perdono, una prospettiva psicoanalitica intergenerazionale, Raffaello Cortina Publisher, Milan.

[66] For further study, see bibliography: Irtelli F. (2021) Sul perdono, l'esperienza umana della rinascita, La Bussola Publisher, Rome.

It must also be specified that those who have been traumatized, even in childhood, have not infrequently experienced emotional and cognitive chaos in their relationship with their abusive parents because it is often as if the abusive parent is suggesting to the child that what he or she is experiencing is not real[67] (clearly to prevent it from being reported); in fact, the abused individual is often left with the paradoxical impression of unreality regarding what he or she is experiencing.[68]

The victim of abuse then feels that what has happened cannot be told to anyone, except by running the risk of being considered insane and finding himself or herself in a state of complete loneliness: the mind of the sufferer may then accumulate a series of primitive and inexpressible contents[69] (thus unprocessed).

In this regard, Cesare Albasi delves into cases of abuse in which unhealthy relationships are created, characterized by "traumatic attachments," that is, ties to an attachment figure that does not confirm the subjective experience but rather contributes to emotional chaos. In traumatic attachment relationships, dissociated internal operating models are often created, which hinder the formulations of the subjective meaning of the vicissitudes central to the attachment experience, disrupting the understanding of their course, intimacy, and thus the possibility of establishing relationships. This lack of meaning can also distort the development of attachment relationships through short-circuiting even harmful actions.[70]

Traumatic bonding can also be solidified through manipulative and contradictory messages, for example, convincing those abused to do something for their own interests by communicating that, instead, "you are only doing it for your own good." Regardless of the age of those subjected to the abuse, those being manipulated generally feel guilty until they do what the manipulator wants.[71]

[67] For further discussion, see bibliography: Albasi C. (2012) Attaccamenti traumatici: modeli operativi interni dissociati, UTET, Turin University, Turin; Albasi C. (2012) Dissociated Internal Working Models: A relational perspective on attachment, trauma and dissociation, Nova Science Publishers Inc, New York.

[68] For further study, see bibliography: Irtelli F. (2021) Sul perdono, l'esperienza umana della rinascita, La Bussola Publisher, Rome.

[69] For more details, see bibliography: previous note.

[70] For further discussion, see the bibliography: Albasi C. (2012) Traumatic attachments: the dissociated internal operating models, UTET, University, Turin.

[71] For further study, see bibliography: Irtelli F. (2021) Sul perdono, l'esperienza umana della rinascita, La Bussola Publisher, Rome.

Thus, in the wake of these dynamics, a relationship of dependence is established in which one ends up annulling oneself and neglecting one's own needs, in favor of those of the manipulator. These processes are characteristic of the victim's affective attachment to the offender,[72] which is a bond that may seem paradoxical (if not even sado-masochistic): in reality, it is the relationship that is established between a dependent person (also due to low self-esteem) and the person on whom he/she depends; it should also be specified that affective attachment is most frequently created in childhood (but not only).

Childhood is the age when the child, in order to relate to the environment, needs an adult person; however, a similar attachment may also arise in adulthood, when, for example, the situation turns out to be out of the ordinary: in much rarer cases, this may occur during an abduction, in which case the affective attachment to the assailant is commonly referred to as Stockholm Syndrome.[73] "Traumatic attachments," that is, unhealthy relationships between victims and assailants, can thus be established and can be mistaken *for feelings of sympathy, empathy or even love.*[74]

Despite the similarities between this type of attachment (e.g., in the cases of those who become engaged with the abductor) and the feelings related to forgiveness, it must be specified that there is a fundamental difference: in unhealthy attachment, the victim, whether a child or an adult, manifests a loss of self-awareness and otherness, which are necessary prerequisites for having a healthy relationship.[75]

Even when considering situations far from extreme (such as those linking the victim to the abductor), it is clear that, in these kinds of toxic relationships, the presence of such an attachment system is not conducive

[72] For further study, see bibliography: Irtelli F. (2021) Sul perdono, l'esperienza umana della rinascita, La Bussola Publisher, Rome. See also Barcaccia B., Mancini F. (2013) Teoria e clinica del perdono, Raffaello Cortina, Milan.

[73] For more details, see the bibliography: Biagini V. Zeonbi S., Vargas M., Marasco M. (2010) The Stockholm Syndrome: media phenomenon or psychiatric pathology? Italian Journal of Criminology, 4 (2) 379–387.

[74] It has happened that people abducted for political reasons have returned home affiliated with their abductors, one may wonder if under the influence of Stockholm Syndrome: this is a psychic issue in which those who manifest the syndrome idealize those who actually committed abuse.

[75] For further study see bibliography: Irtelli F. (2021) Sul perdono, l'esperienza umana della rinascita, La Bussola Publisher, Rome.

to the maintenance of a broad, fluid, lucid, and continuous consciousness—in short, healthy.[76]

These considerations underscore how relational dynamics must be focused on from multiple perspectives: as clinicians, we must keep in mind that in the "relational system," we must go beyond just the trauma complained of but rather push ourselves to explore the various aspects of the relational functioning of the subject and those with whom the subject interacts.

It is therefore appropriate, in other words, to focus on relational dynamics from a perspective according to which we need to go beyond trauma alone but rather push ourselves to explore the various aspects of the functioning of each individual involved in the scenario and their interlocking with each other.

Critical issues that may be encountered in this trauma reprocessing course may subsist in the fact that often, those who seek help in coping with a traumatic event bring only the urgency to "turn off the pain," but it is also appropriate to observe all the dynamics that contextualize the trauma experience, such as irrational guilt, "negative attachment," "death drive," and "traumatic attachments." It is fair to specify that it is dangerous to generalize the course after trauma, as there are significant variations among people, types of trauma, and the environment in which the trauma takes place, so the dynamics just summarized may or may not occur.

Beyond Trauma

Some time ago, a mother came for counseling to talk about her daughter, who exhibited very troubling behaviors manifested by repeated antisocial actions. The history revealed the existence of a second male child, which had nothing to do with the request for psychological counseling; he was an unwanted child, according to the mother, "unwanted from the beginning."

Thus, the infant had been in the care of his grandparents until shortly after his birth and had returned to his family of origin at home with his already growing father and mother. This child had been abused by a neighbor of the grandparents, a person against whom a complaint was filed. The mother says that the boy to date appears to be in good health

[76] For further study, see the bibliography: Liotti G. (2005) The interpersonal dimension of consciousness, Carocci editore, Rome p. 231.

and that he recently left the parental home and found a good job and a loving partner to live with. The other daughter, on the other hand, for whom the mother sought counseling, was described as highly desired and sought after, raised surrounded by her parents' affection: she had better chances for development, yet she presented a great many problems, was very unstable, and even dangerous.

The idea that trauma can definitely create a permanent deviation in an individual's life course with 100% probability is certainly to be questioned; the truth is that every reaction is subjective: even those who have suffered severe shocks can continue to live normally, and on the other hand, those who grow up in a protective and resourceful environment can also evolve in a fragile and problematic way. It should also be specified that, for another thing, it is *not* inevitable that trauma with enormous magnitude will still create a chronic outcome. Investigations conducted on populations of concentration camp survivors fifty years later have revealed that many people have some intrusive memories of the trauma and some avoidance phenomena of trauma-related stimuli but are not affected by post-traumatic stress disorder; in fact, exposure to trauma is a necessary but not sufficient factor to explain the onset of chronic symptoms.[77] Finally, it should be noted that everyone responds in his or her own way to life events, and we must remember that this is influenced by various biological, psychological, and social factors: there may be conditioning from one's history, temperament, and social context, but everyone is free to contradict these conditioning; in fact, each life trajectory is never completely predictable, so each course of psychotherapy is unique.

[77] For further discussion, see bibliography: Williams R. ed. (2009) Trauma e relazioni, le prospettive scientifiche e cliniche contemporenee, Raffaello Cortina Publisher, Milan.

CHAPTER 2

Fragility After Trauma

Abstract This chapter highlights that PTSD is a complex and varied disorder that can be associated with other psychiatric disorders, particularly depression, with which it can have a comorbid relationship; PTSD can also be associated with personality, eating, dissociative, antisocial, and aggressive disorders, as well as with increased suicide risk and physical health problems. The chapter also reviews studies showing that children and adolescents can also develop PTSD following traumatic events, and we have described the specific diagnostic criteria for children, which have peculiarities compared with adults. Having made this premise, we have described some tests and scales used to assess PTSD and the impact of trauma, both in adults and children, and we have highlighted the importance of also assessing trauma exposure, the etiology of the disorder, the patient's history, and his or her adjustment levels.

Keywords PTSD • Depression • Comorbid relationship • Diagnosis • Children • Adults • Epidemiology

Trauma and Frailty in Adults

We observed in Chap. 1, what is now called posttraumatic stress disorder in scientific terms is represented by a constellation of symptoms, both psychological and physical, whose identification within a univocal clinical

© The Author(s), under exclusive license to Springer Nature Switzerland AG 2024

F. Irtelli, F. Gabrielli, *Contemporary Perspectives on Trauma and Resilience*, https://doi.org/10.1007/978-3-031-70793-3_2

picture is not always simple. On the one hand, we are facilitated in identifying PTSD because the underlying cause is usually obvious; on the other hand, we are faced with a very complex phenomenon, both because of the variety of symptoms and because of the many biological and psychological processes involved.

This psychopathological picture also often appears to be associated with other disorders, as after exposure to a traumatic experience, PTSD is not the only psychiatric condition that can develop; anxiety, substance abuse, and depression can also arise,[1] and comorbidity is the norm rather than the exception.[2]

In this regard, depression has been found to be one of the most severe and prevalent conditions occurring in conjunction with PTSD,[3] and it has long been known that depression is the disorder that occurs most frequently in association with PTSD.[4] In fact, even from research conducted as early as the 1990s following natural and technological disasters, a high frequency of depressive symptoms after a disaster clearly appeared.[5]

Having observed the frequency of comorbidity, several studies have been carried out since the 1990s to determine more precisely the relationship between depression and PTSD, and in this regard, it has been observed that if, prior to the trauma, an individual already had PTSD or depressive episodes, the individual was more predisposed to develop the

[1] For further discussion, see bibliography: Williams R. ed. (2009) Trauma e relazioni, le prospettive scientifiche e cliniche contemporenee, Raffaello Cortina Publisher, Milan.

[2] For further discussion, see the bibliography: O'Donnell M.L., Creamer M., Pattison P. (2004) *Posttraumatic Stress Disorder and Depression Following Trauma: Understanding Comorbidity, Am J Psychiatry*, 161:1390–1396; Durbano F., Marchesi B., Irtelli F. (2024) *Perspective Chapter: Trauma and Depression—an Overview about comorbidity.* In Depression what is new and what is old in human existence, Intehcopen, London.

[3] For further discussion, see bibliography: Creamer M., Burgess P., McFarlane A.C. (2001) *Posttraumatic stress disorder: findings from the Australian National Survey of Mental Health and Well-Being.* Psychol Med, 31:1237–1247.

[4] For further discussion see bibliography: O'Donnell M.L., Creamer M., (2004) Pattison, *Posttraumatic Stress Disorder and Depression Following Trauma: Understanding Comorbidity,* American Journal of Psychiatry (2004); 161:1390–1396.

[5] For further discussion see bibliography: Green B.L. (1994) *Traumatic Stress and Disaster, mental health effects and factors influencing adaptation,* in: Liehmac F., Nadelson C., International Review of Psychiatry, vol 2. American Psychiatric press, Washington, DC (1994).

pathology of the two not previously experienced, as it appears that each of the two disorders predisposes to vulnerability to the other.[6]

Scientific studies have suggested that over time, depressive symptoms are often an integral part of PTSD and that identifying depression as a distinct PTSD disorder sometimes appears to be a daunting task; however, there is also evidence to suggest that depression after trauma may also exist as a separate and independent entity.[7]

In summary, after exposure to trauma, PTSD and depression can manifest either as separate disorders or as concomitant disorders, and some scholars have raised the question of whether PTSD and depression are part of a single overarching construct, even suggesting upstream that when PTSD and depression occur together, these disorders reflect a shared vulnerability with similar predictor variables.[8]

Further investigation of the correlation between posttraumatic experiences and depression revealed that for women facing pregnancy in adulthood, previous traumatic events are a risk factor for developing postpartum depression,[9] and the relationship between trauma and postpartum depression has also been noted; in particular, traumatic events experienced in the military may increase the risk of postpartum depression among women who are more likely to have faced posttraumatic experiences during the course of military service.[10]

Regarding the relationship between depression and posttraumatic experiences, it is also worth noting that it has been reported that some

[6] For further discussion, see bibliography: O'Donnell M.L., Creamer M., Pattison (2004) *Posttraumatic Stress Disorder and Depression Following Trauma: Understanding Comorbidity,* American Journal of Psychiatry 161:1390–1396.

[7] For further discussion, see the bibliography: O'Donnell M.L., Creamer M., Pattison P. (2004) *Posttraumatic Stress Disorder and Depression Following Trauma: Understanding Comorbidity, Am J Psychiatry,* 161:1390–1396.

[8] For further discussion, see the bibliography: O'Donnell M.L., Creamer M., Pattison P. (2004) *Posttraumatic Stress Disorder and Depression Following Trauma: Understanding Comorbidity,* Am J Psychiatry, 161:1390–1396.

[9] For more details, see the bibliography: Alvarez-Segura M., Garcia-Esteve L., Torres A., Plaza A., Imaz M. L., Hermida-Barros L., San L., Burtchen N. (2014) *Are women with a history of abuse more vulnerable to perinatal depressive symptoms? A systematic review.* Archives of Women's Mental Health, 17(5), 343–357. doi: https://doi.org/10.1007/s00737-014-0440-9.

[10] For further discussion, see the bibliography: Combellick J.L. et al. (2020): *Postpartum Depression in a Cohort of Post-9/11 Women Veterans: The Role of MilitaryStress and Trauma,* Military Behavioral Health, DOI: https://doi.org/10.1080/21635781.2020.1751351.

women diagnosed with postpartum depression experienced childbirth itself as a trauma and then continued to experience negative thoughts and emotions for a long time; this factor was found to be predictive of the development of depression.[11] This event is not uncommon; in fact, approximately one in three women rate their childbirth experience as traumatic.

It should be pointed out, upstream of all this, that posttraumatic stress disorder can often distort the cognitions of the person experiencing it, and in fact, it is typically a disorder that involves a perception of the self as vulnerable, a perception of the world as unreliable, and a fear of the future as unpredictable. We can also observe, at this point, that depression shares with posttraumatic experiences some major categories of symptoms (which may fall under perception distortions), such as irrational feelings of fear for the future; other symptoms in common with PTSD may be sleep disturbances and difficulties in concentrating, which in turn induce negative thoughts and emotions and can be generalized and expanded to imply a perception of the self in failed terms, a catastrophic worldview and a perception of the future as hopeless.[12]

We must also point out that even several depressive episodes begin as a consequence of a trauma, of a loss, which can be a bereavement but also the loss of a social position, of an autonomy, the loss of a role, all factors that were considered essential for the subject and for the maintenance of his or her psychic balance, and these events can be experienced precisely as a trauma, regardless of whether they caused PTSD or not. We can assert that after a traumatic event, whatever it may be, it is, however, not always an easy task to purely diagnose depression to a subject who requires psychological counseling because of a long-standing suffering that he or she cannot fully define, since depressive disorder, such as PTSD, presents itself with various signs and may become confused with other symptoms. It therefore seems very important to make an accurate diagnosis both to initiate psychotherapy and to introduce possible pharmacological support.[13]

[11] For further study, see bibliography: Caretti V., Capraro G. (2008) *Trauma and psychopathology*, Astrolabio Ubaldini, Rome.

[12] For further study, see bibliography: Caretti V., Capraro G. (2008) *Trauma and psychopathology*, Astrolabio Ubaldini, Rome.

[13] For more details, see the bibliography: Zacchetti E. Castelnuovo G. (2021) *Il trattamento della depressione tra illusioni e speranze, esperienze e interventi in psicologia clinica,* Franco Angeli Publisher, Milan.

All these considerations about the intertwining of trauma and depression lead us to consider, as anticipated above, that depression can make one more vulnerable to PTSD and that PTSD can make one more vulnerable to depression because the two disorders appear to be interrelated.[14] However, we must emphasize that the symptoms of each of the two disorders also have their own peculiarities and specificities; for example, in PTSD, intrusive memories are distinct from the mental rumination typical of depression in that they apply only to involuntary, intrusive unpleasant memories concerning the trauma.[15]

Posttraumatic Stress Disorder and Comorbidity in Adults

For no apparent reason did I feel suddenly crushed by a crescendo of insane and irrational fear, which defied all logic of discernment (...); nothing that General Galtieri's men had caused was in any way comparable to the terror that my own mind generated that evening. Since I had seen death in the face on a wind-swept isthmus near Gus Green and, two weeks later, again on a bare hill called Wireless Ridge, I think I can honestly say that I was no longer afraid of death or of the things, real or imagined, that are normally the subject of phobias. That night I had seen the terror of the only thing that could still scare me, which was myself. I was terrified of losing control.[16]

Huges S., 1990, p. 1476

We have already emphasized the frequency and importance of the comorbidity of PTSD with depression, but we should point out that people who are victims of severe trauma may also experience permanent personality changes (e.g., developing personality disorders); conversely, if personality disorders already exist, they may in turn make the subject more

[14] For further discussion, see the bibliography: O'Donnell M.L., Creamer M., Pattison, *Posttraumatic Stress Disorder and Depression Following Trauma: Understanding Comorbidity*, American Journal of Psychiatry (2004); 161:1390–1396; Durbano F., Marchesi B., Irtelli F. (2024) *Perspective Chapter: Trauma and Depression—an Overview about comorbidity*. In Depression what is new and what is old in human existence, Intehcopen, London.

[15] For more details, see the bibliography: American Psychiatric Association, DSM-5 Task Force. (2013). Diagnostic and Statistical Manual of Mental Disorders: DSM-5™ (5th ed.). American Psychiatric Publishing, Inc, Washington DC, it. Trad. (2014) Raffaello Cortina Editore, Milan.

[16] For further discussion see bibliography: Hughes S. (1990) *Inside madness*. In British Medical Journal, 301, pp. 1476–1478.

vulnerable to PTSD.[17] Eating disorders, dissociative episodes of varying degrees, and antisocial and aggressive manifestations have also been found by other studies to be associated with PTSD.[18]

It also appears that individuals with PTSD may manifest an increased suicidal risk (especially if they have a diagnosis showing comorbidity with depression).[19]

After a posttraumatic experience, moreover, physical health may be compromised in various other ways: in general there is an increased incidence of asthenia, headaches, chest pain, and gastrointestinal and cardiovascular disorders.[20] Undoubtedly, many of these physical signs are also common to depression, and given the relevance and frequency of the topic of depression in comorbidity associated with posttraumatic experiences this topic will be the subject of the third chapter.

Trauma, Frailty, and Comorbidity in Developmental Age

We should specify that although the diagnosis of PTSD, when it was first formulated in 1980, was not considered relevant to children and adolescents at the time, Leonore Terr's studies of a group of children who were kidnapped and held hostage proved otherwise.[21] Unfortunately, it is also well known that adults often underestimate the severity of children's reactions to trauma and may therefore be unaware of children's need to

[17] For further discussion, see bibliography: Horowitz M. J. (2004) Sindrome da stress: valutazione e trattamento. Raffaello Cortina Publisher, Milan.

[18] For further study, see bibliography: Sgarro M. (1998) Post Traumatic Stress Disorder, aspetti clinici e psicoterapie. Kappa, Rome.

[19] For further discussion, see bibliography: Oquendo M.A., Friend J.M, Batsheva Halberstam B.A., Brodsky B.S. (2003) *Association of Comorbid Posttraumatic Stress Disorder and Major Depression With Greater Risk for Suicidal Behavior*, American Journal of Psychiatry, 160: 580–582, March.

[20] For further discussion, see bibliography: Sutker P.B., Uddo-Crane M., Allain A. (1991) *Clinical and research assessment of posttraumatic stress disorder: a conceptual overview*, A Journal of Consulting and Clinical Psychology, 3, 4, 520–530.

[21] For further study, see bibliography: Terr, L.C. (1979). Children of Chowchilla. *A study of psychic terror*. The Psychoanalytic Study of the Child, 34, 547–623. Terr, L.C. (1983). Chowchilla revisited: *The effect of psychic trauma four years after a school-bus kidnapping*. American Journal of Psychiatry, 140, 1543–1550.

reprocess their experience.[22] In the scientific community, on the other hand, it is now clear that minors can also develop PTSD (and other disorders) following traumatic events; thus, several studies have been carried out in this regard,[23,24] although it is fair to point out that most epidemiological studies on PTSD have been conducted mostly on adolescents and adults rather than on children. On the other hand, diagnosis with young children can be particularly complex and challenging: in fact, it has been observed that young children have more trouble reporting avoidance reactions because they are not relevant or too complicated to put into words since they require rather articulate cognitive introspection, which can make it more difficult for young children to meet the DSM criterion of avoidance.[25]

The diagnosis of PTSD in children over the age of six and adolescents is almost isomorphic to the basic criteria that apply to adults, whereas for infants under the age of six the diagnosis, as anticipated, can be difficult and has its own peculiarity.[26] It must be based on the following criteria:

1. Exposure to actual or threatened death, serious injury, or sexual assault in one of the following ways: directly experiencing the traumatic event, directly witnessing trauma occurring to others, or learning of the trauma occurring to a family member (or to a caregiver figure). The trauma must have occurred in one or more of the above ways.

[22] For further discussion, see bibliography: Dyregrov A., Yule W., (2005) *A Review of PTSD in Children, Child and Adolescent Mental Health* Vol. 11, No. 4, 2006, pp. 176–184, doi: https://doi.org/10.1111/j.1475-3588.2005.00384.x_ 2005.

[23] For further study, see bibliography: Terr, L.C. (1979). *Children of Chowchilla. A study of psychic terror.* The Psychoanalytic Study of the Child, 34, 547–623. Terr, L.C. (1983). Chowchilla revisited: The effect of psychic trauma four years after a school-bus kidnapping. American Journal of Psychiatry, 140, 1543–1550.

[24] For further discussion, see bibliography: Dyregrov A., Yule W. (2005) *A Review of PTSD in Children, Child and Adolescent Mental Health* Vol. 11, No. 4, 2006, pp. 176–184, doi: https://doi.org/10.1111/j.1475-3588.2005.00384.x_ 2005.

[25] For further discussion, see bibliography: Dyregrov A., Yule W. (2005) *A Review of PTSD in Children, Child and Adolescent Mental Health* Vol. 11, No. 4, 2006, pp. 176–184, doi: https://doi.org/10.1111/j.1475-3588.2005.00384.x_ 2005.

[26] For further discussion, see bibliography: American Psychiatric Association, DSM-5 Task Force (2013). Diagnostic and Statistical Manual of Mental Disorders: DSM-5™ (5th ed.). American Psychiatric Publishing, Inc, Washington DC, it. Trad. (2014) Raffaello Cortina Editore, Milan.

2. Presence of one or more of the following intrusive symptoms: recurrent, involuntary, unpleasant memories of the trauma. Recurrent unpleasant dreams related to the trauma. Dissociative reactions, for example, *flashbacks*, in which the child feels or acts as if the trauma is recurring (this may occur during play). Intense or prolonged psychological distress upon exposure to internal or external triggers that symbolize or resemble some aspect of the trauma. Marked physiological reactions in response to factors reminiscent of the trauma.
3. One or more of the following symptoms represent persistent avoidance of trauma-associated stimuli or negative alterations in emotions and thoughts: persistent avoidance of trauma-related stimuli, negative alterations such as an increased frequency of negative emotional states, a marked decrease in interest or participation in meaningful activities, withdrawn social behavior, and persistent reduction in the expression of positive emotions.
4. Altered reactivity associated with trauma: irritable behavior and anger outbursts, hypervigilance, exaggerated alarm responses, concentration problems, and sleep-related difficulties.
5. The duration of the alterations was longer than one month.
6. Impairment causes clinically significant clinical distress (impairment in relationships with parents, siblings, peers, or others).[27]

It should be noted that for children younger than the age of six, unlike adults, re-experiencing trauma-related events may occur during play, which directly or symbolically refers to the trauma, and in younger children, it is also possible for developmental regression to occur due to post-traumatic stress disorder, such as loss of language use.[28] Young children may also report a new onset of frightening dreams without specific content related to the traumatic event, and parents may experience a wide range of emotional and behavioral changes. Because of infants' limited ability to

[27] For further discussion, see bibliography: American Psychiatric Association, DSM-5 Task Force. (2013). Diagnostic and Statistical Manual of Mental Disorders: DSM-5™ (5th ed.). American Psychiatric Publishing, Inc, Washington DC, it. Trad. (2014) Raffaello Cortina Editore, Milan.

[28] For further discussion, see bibliography: American Psychiatric Association, DSM-5 Task Force. (2013). Diagnostic and Statistical Manual of Mental Disorders: DSM-5™ (5th ed.). American Psychiatric Publishing, Inc, Washington DC, it. Trad. (2014) Raffaello Cortina Editore, Milan.

express thoughts or categorize emotions, negative mood and thought alterations tend to involve mainly mood changes. In older school-age children, on the other hand, reduced participation in new activities may be found; in adolescents, reluctance to seek developmental opportunities such as learning to drive or participating in social gatherings may also be manifested. After trauma, adolescents may harbor the belief that they have changed in ways that make them socially undesirable and lose their aspirations for the future. Moreover, in adolescents, the irritable and aggressive behavior triggered after trauma may interfere with relationships with peers and behavior at school.[29]

As we have observed, the clinical expression of re-experiencing a traumatic event can vary through different developmental stages; in fact, following exposure to traumatic stressors, people show a wide range of stress reactions, and these reactions vary with age and, to some extent, also by sex. It has been noted that after trauma, younger children may show more repetitive play (and drawings) about the traumatic event as well as behavioral reenactments. For preschoolers, there is also less agreement on the extent and severity of their reactions to stress, and for this age group, reactions appear to be more determined by parental reactions to the event: if parents respond calmly, the child may in fact feel more protected and secure. Above the age of six, on the other hand, as anticipated, children's reactions become more similar to those manifested by adults: the school-age child is better able to understand the situation, is able to see to a greater extent the long-term consequences of the traumatic event(s), and can reflect more on his or her own role in what happened. Gender differences often appear in the reactions of children and adolescents: more girls than boys qualify for PTSD diagnosis, while boys show higher rates of behavioral symptoms.[30]

It should be specified that there are also numerous studies regarding childhood trauma and the development of depression, again highlighting a strong correlation between trauma and depression. Indeed, it has been found that trauma symptoms and depression symptoms are again

[29] For further discussion, see bibliography: American Psychiatric Association, DSM-5 Task Force. (2013). Diagnostic and Statistical Manual of Mental Disorders: DSM-5™ (5th ed.). American Psychiatric Publishing, Inc, Washington DC, it. Trad. (2014) Raffaello Cortina Editore, Milan.

[30] For further discussion, see bibliography: Yule W., Perrin S., Smith, P. (1999). *Posttraumatic stress reactions in children and adolescents.* In W. Yule (Ed.). *Posttraumatic stress disorders: Concepts and therapy.* Chichester: John Wiley & Sons.

positively correlated with each other: traumatized children and adolescents who had a stronger belief that they would be killed during an accident reported higher levels of both posttraumatic symptoms and depression within one month of the trauma.[31]

There is now a growing awareness that childhood trauma is also a major risk factor for the development of depressive disorders in adulthood; indeed, it has been reported that traumatized people may be more susceptible to the adverse effects of subsequent stressors.[32]

In this regard, several in-depth studies of young subjects have shown that physiological upset immediately after exposure to trauma can predict anxiety and depression,[33] and it has been observed and confirmed that childhood trauma is associated with the onset of depression in adulthood.[34] It appears, in this regard, that there is indeed a specific relationship between childhood trauma and the subsequent development of depression: one study revealed a fourfold increase in the risk of depression in adults who had experienced multiple traumas during childhood[35] and the role of childhood trauma in the development of depression.[36]

Finally, it appears that individuals who have experienced early trauma themselves seem to be particularly susceptible to the depressive effects of

[31] For further discussion, see bibliography: Ellis A. A., Nixon R. D., Williamson P. *The effects of social support and negative appraisals on acute stress symptoms and depression in children and adolescents.* British Journal of Psychology. 2009;48:347–361.

[32] For further discussion, see the bibliography: Heim C., Newport D.J., Mletzko T., Miller A.H., C. B. Nemeroff (2008) *The link between childhood trauma and depression: Insights from HPA axis studies in humans*, Psychoneuroendocrinology 33, 693–710.

[33] For further discussion, see bibliography: Barber B.A., Kohl K.L., Kassam-Adams N., Gold J.I. (2014) *Acute stress, depression, and anxiety symptoms among English and Spanish speaking children with recent trauma exposure, Journal of Clin Psychol Med Settings.* 2014 March; 21(1): 66–71. doi: https://doi.org/10.1007/s10880-013-9382-z.

[34] For further discussion, see bibliography: Gladstone G.L., Parker G.B., Mitchell P.B., Malhi G.S., Wilhelm et al., (2004) *Implications of childhood trauma for depressed women: an analysis of pathways from childhood sexual abuse to deliberate self-harm and revictimization.* Am. J. Psychiatry 161, 1417–1425.

[35] For further discussion, see bibliography: Felitti V.J., Anda R.F., Nordenberg D., Williamson D.F., Spitz A.M., Edwards V., Koss M.P., Marks J.S., (1998) *Relationship of childhood abuse and household dysfunction to many of the leading causes of death in adults. The Adverse Childhood Experiences (ACE) Study.* Am. J. Prev. Med. 14, 245–258.

[36] For further discussion, see the bibliography: Nelson E.C., Heath A.C., Madden P.A., Cooper M.L., Dinwiddie S.H., Bucholz K.K., Glowinski A., McLaughlin T., Dunne M.P., Statham D.J., Martin N.G. (2002) *Association between self-reported childhood sexual abuse and adverse psychosocial outcomes: results from a twin study.* Arch. Gen. Psychiatry 59, 139–145.

acute stress in adulthood:[37] physiological upset immediately after exposure to trauma has been shown to be a sensitive predictor of subsequent symptoms of stress, depression, and emotional numbing.[38]

Regarding the issue of comorbidity, it is also worth specifying that regardless of age, children exposed to chronic and repeated stressors, such as physical and sexual abuse, war, or molestation, may develop personality changes, various self-injurious and suicidal behaviors, depression, or other psychiatric disorders. Exposure to trauma in childhood can also affect the maturation of the central nervous system and neuroendocrine system; a review of neurobiological sequelae can be found in research by van der Kolk.[39] Many of the neuroendocrine findings reported in the literature for patients with major depression appear to be secondary to early childhood stress, likely representing a psychobiological risk for the development of depression in response to stress. Other risk factors, such as female sex and genetic dispositions, may interfere with the components of the stress response and thus further increase vulnerability to depression in relation to childhood trauma.[40]

Finally, it should be specified that not all individuals exposed to early childhood adversity will eventually develop depression and/or posttraumatic stress disorder, even after further episodes of stress or challenge; therefore, the "upstream" moderating effects of biological dispositional factors,[41] social support[42] and possible psychotherapy should also always be considered in the assessment phase.

[37] For further discussion, see bibliography: Kendler, K.S., Kuhn, J.W., Prescott, C.A. (2004) *Childhood sexual abuse, stressful life events and risk for major depression in women.* Psychol. Med. 34, 1475–1482.

[38] For further discussion, see bibliography: Barber B.A., Kohl K.L., Kassam-Adams N., Gold J.I. (2014) *Acute stress, depression, and anxiety symptoms among English and Spanish speaking children with recent trauma exposure Journal of Clin Psychol Med Settings.* 21(1): 66–71. doi: https://doi.org/10.1007/s10880-013-9382-z.

[39] For further discussion, see bibliography: van der Kolk B. (2003) *The neurobiology of childhood trauma and abuse. Child and Adolescent Psychiatric Clinics of North America, 12,* 293–317.

[40] For further discussion, see bibliography: Heim C., Newport D.J., Mletzko T., Miller A.H., Nemeroff C.B. (2008) *The link between childhood trauma and depression: Insights from HPA axis studies in humans,* Psychoneuroendocrinology 33, 693–710.

[41] For further discussion, see bibliography: Heim C., Newport D.J., Mletzko T., Miller A.H., Nemeroff C.B. (2008) *The link between childhood trauma and depression: Insights from HPA axis studies in humans,* Psychoneuroendocrinology 33, 693–710.

[42] For further discussion, see bibliography: Ellis AA, Nixon RD, Williamson P. *The effects of social support and negative appraisals on acute stress symptoms and depression in children and adolescents.* British Journal of Psychology, 2009; 48: 347–361.

There is now an awareness both that the consequences of trauma experienced by minor individuals can spill over into their psychological development and that various environmental, interpersonal, and individual factors can have negative or preventative influences with respect to the onset of psychopathology. We can consider, for example, that mistreatment by one parent of a child may have less impact if the other parental figure is more appropriate, just as we know that sometimes a peer group that is highly adapted to provide emotional support can reduce the psychological effects of an abusive home environment.

Possible Diagnostic Pictures

The need to take into account the complexity of PTSD and possible comorbidities has been emphasized; therefore, the use of multiple diagnoses is a valuable element in the treatment of stress response syndromes, particularly PTSD.[43]

Making an accurate diagnosis and taking into account the difficulties involved is important for designing an appropriate therapeutic intervention.

Therefore, great attention must be given to clinical diagnosis, where it must be distinguished whether the diagnosis of PTSD is secondary or primary to parallel codiagnoses. Examples of tests used to identify PTSD include *the MMPI-2-Post-Traumatic Stress Disorder Scale* and the *Posttraumatic Stress Disorder Symptom Scale (PSS)*.[44]

[43] For further discussion, see the bibliography: Horowitz M.J. (2004), *Stress response syndromes, assessment and treatment.* Raffaello Cortina, Milan.

[44] We also recall among the tests aimed at detecting PTSD the following standardized self-reports: *Raction Index*, consisting of twenty items (modest validity); *NWS PTSD Module*, consisting of twenty items (proven validity); *PPS*, consisting of seventy items (proven validity); Purdure PTSD Scale, consisting of seventeen items (modest validity); *PTSD interview*, consisting of twenty items (proven validity); Civilian Mississipi, consisting of thirty-five items (modest validity); *Revised Mississipi, consisting of* thirty items (modest validity); Penn Inventory, consisting of twenty-six items (intermediate validity); TSC 40, consisting of forty items (moderate validity); *Trauma Symptom Inventory*, consisting of hundred items (intermediate validity*); Harvard Trauma Questionnaire-symptoms*, consisting of thirty items (proven validity) (Wilson et al., 1997); mention also the more recent *PCLS: Post-Traumatic Checklist Scale*, a short self-report questionnaire; apparently it has good psychometric properties and is useful for screening and assessment of this disorder. For more details see the bibliography: Yao S.N., Cottraux J., De Mey-Guillard C., Mollard E., Ventureyra V., (2003) *Evaluation of Posttraumatic stress disorder: validation of a measure, the PCLS.* Encephale, May-Jun 29 (3pt): 232–238.

To assess PTSD in children, the *Child PTSD Symptom* Scale was created: a seventeen-item scale developed by Edna Foa and collaborators,[45] which has been used in both initial diagnosis and progress monitoring and allows for a brief assessment of functional impairment.

Instead, to assess the impact of trauma more generally, the adult scale "*The Impact of Event* Scale" was created[46] and later adapted for use with children and adolescents.[47]

For the assessment of PTSD, it is also necessary to assess exposure to trauma and examine the etiology of the disturbance: this is usually done in the context of a retrospective *self-report* and during a clinical interview[48] in which the identification of clinical cases of PTSD is important, that is, to establish the threshold for detecting the presence of the disorder or not, a task that is very complicated due to the presence of subclinical diagnostic pictures or characterized by comorbidities.

A clinical interview, characterized by a systematic collection of information, is one of the most popular tools for obtaining information for the purpose of diagnosis and the creation of a therapeutic plan; to design a therapeutic intervention, it is also usually desirable to investigate the patient's pretrauma history and his or her adjustment levels, supplementing them, if possible, with information provided by the person closest to the patient.[49]

As anticipated in Chap. 1, it should also be remembered that the onset of disorders following severe traumatic events may occur within a time frame distant from the traumatic episode; for this reason, it is often necessary to implement longitudinal observations of patients who have experienced traumatic events.

[45] For further discussion, see the bibliography: Foa E.B., Johnson, K.M., Feeny, N.C., & Treadwell, K.R.H. (2001). The Child PTSD Symptom Scale: A preliminary examination of its psychometric properties. *Journal of Community Psychology*, *30*, 376–384.

[46] For further discussion, see bibliography: Horowitz M., Wilner, N., Alvarez, W. (1979) *Impact of Event Scale: A measure of subjective stress. Psychosomatic Medicine*, *41*, 209–218.

[47] For further discussion, see the bibliography: Yule W. (1997) *Anxiety, depression and post-traumatic stress in childhood*, Child Psychology Portfolio. London: NFER-NELSON.

[48] For further study, see the bibliography: Wilson J.P., Keane T.M. (1997) *Assessing psychological trauma and PTSD*, Guilford Press, New York London.

[49] For further discussion, see the bibliography: Yule W. (2000) *Post-Traumatic Stress Disorder, aspetti clinici e terapia*, McGraw Hill, Milan.

In the case of assessment with children, it may be useful to focus on the child's trauma experience as early as the first session; the use of systematic assessment of both the child's exposure to the trauma and its effects should be incorporated into a clinical interview in which the child or adolescent can describe his or her experience with a wealth of clinical information that can determine the choice of therapy. For single traumas, it is advisable to provide the child from the very first session with help (i.e., a simple method of reducing intrusive thoughts) to help him or her with his or her most troublesome symptoms; this can increase the patient's optimism and motivation to return. When meeting and assessing a child, drawing can also be used as a communication tool. If children are given the opportunity to draw about an emotionally charged event while talking about it, children between the ages of three and nine report more detailed verbal accounts than when they are asked to give an account without drawing.[50]

As already specified, both in the case of adults and in the case of children and adolescents, the diagnosis of PTSD, such as depression, is complex, articulated on several phenomenological planes. Therefore, it is important, at the diagnostic stage, to have clear cognitions about the syndromic grouping of disorders; in this regard, a number of studies concerning the procedures and criteria for differentiating between PTSD and other psychopathological forms appeared in the 1990s.[51]

Diagnostic differentiation is not always easy; we refer, for example, to the 'pregnancy setting,' of which we observed clinical cases in Chap. 1: in the pregnancy setting, many misdiagnoses of postnatal depression or adjustment problems have been made on women who actually suffer from PTSD, leading to the choice of inappropriate treatments. For this reason, it is appropriate to use two different instruments in this specific case to distinguish mothers suffering from postnatal depression (in this case, the most suitable logical text instrument is the *Edinburgh Postnatal Depression Scale*) and mothers with more specific PTSD symptoms (for whom the *PTSD Symptom Scale* is particularly suitable).[52]

[50] For further discussion, see bibliography: Dyregrov A., Yule W., (2005) A Review of PTSD in Children, *Child and Adolescent Mental Health* Vol. 11, No. 4, 2006, pp. 176–184, doi: https://doi.org/10.1111/j.1475-3588.2005.00384.x_ 2005.

[51] For further study, see bibliography: Sgarro M. (1998) Post Traumatic Stress Disorder, aspetti clinici e psicoterapie. Kappa, Rome.

[52] For further discussion, see bibliography: Alder J., Staldmayr W., Tschdin S., Bitzerb J. (2006) *Posttraumatic symptoms stress after childbirth: What should we offer?* Journal of Psychosomatic Obstetrics & Gynecology; 27 (2): 107–112.

Common Therapeutic Goals in the Treatment of Traumatized People

In the last three decades, there has been increasing emphasis on mental health pathways for dealing with PTSD;[53] it is clear that in the psychotherapy of trauma patients, it is important that a sense of safety is conveyed, which facilitates people in processing their traumatic experiences (including childhood experiences) and promotes their mentalization. It is also important to try to allow a fading of conceptions altered by the trauma (such as the belief that one is powerless or not worthy of love).

Regarding the specific treatment of the traumatized child, we can say that to prevent a psychopathological outcome at the root, it is important for the traumatized child to be able to talk to adults about the trauma because, in this way,

(a) Restoring experience in memory and preventing forgetting;
(b) Help the child interpret the experience;
(c) Correcting misunderstandings;
(d) Help the child manage and regulate his or her emotions;
(e) Provide information on coping strategies and facilitate their implementation.[54]

Upstream, although there are diverse techniques and approaches for the treatment of PTSD, some similar psychotherapeutic goals are also envisaged for the treatment of PTSD in adults. Meichenbaum,[55] who illustrated the most important psychotherapeutic "guide lines," states as early as the 1990s that the goals may be as follows:

[53] For further discussion, see bibliography: Booysen D.D., Kagee D. (2023) *Trauma survivors' perceptions and experiences of prolonged exposure for PTSD at a psychology clinic*, South African Journal of Psychiatry, p. 1–7. ISSN 2078-6786.

[54] For further discussion, see bibliography: Salmon K., Bryant R.A. (2002) *Posttraumatic stress disorder in children: The influence of developmental factors.* Clinical Psychological Review, 22, 163–188.

[55] For further discussion, see bibliography: Meichenbaum D. *(1994) A clinical handbook/ Practical therapist manual for assessing and treating adults with Post Traumatic Stress Disorder (PTSD),* Institute Press, University of Waterloo, Ontario.

- Helping the patient to reframe his or her story, reliving and recounting the trauma in the "here and now," changing the way it is narrated, to achieve integration and a "sense of control" of the experience. A chance to "find meaning" to the events experienced must also be provided. A sense of mastery of intrusive memories and the ability to tolerate distress can then be achieved through psychotherapy, allowing the patient to relive traumatic memories with a relatively high degree of voluntary control.
- Re-exposing the patient to trauma-related stimuli and signals but in a structured way and with psychological support (e.g., using "direct exposure," various techniques of guided imagination, hypnosis, support, and gradual re-exposure to stresses).
- Focus on beliefs, ideas, and opinions that have been "distorted" in the patient and have caused intrapersonal and interpersonal difficulties: this can occur through cognitive restructuring techniques, problem solving and creative writing. The following can thus be better coped with: guilt, anger, fear, sadness, despair, victimization, and disorientation.
- Starting with the traumatic event itself, personal resources that might underlie growth are examined to move, for example, from the position of victim to that of survivor. To achieve this, it is important to help change the patient's temporal orientation (from a focus on the past to a perspective centered on the present and future); the development of more satisfying lifestyles and closer, stronger social support is thus fostered.
- Spur the patient to activate his or her resources related to the belief system (e.g., religious, philosophical beliefs and convictions).
- The therapist should not provide meaning to the patient, but they should be found by the patient himself, for example, by attending groups of people who have been exposed to the same trauma; it is important to help the person in treatment reconstruct his or her past experience, increasing the feeling of possessing future goals.[56]

[56] For further discussion, see bibliography: Meichenbaum D. (1994) *A clinical handbook/Practical therapist manual for assessing and treating adults with Post Traumatic Stress Disorder (PTSD)*, Institute Press, University of Waterloo, Ontario.

It is also important to remember that Otto Kerberg states that to process trauma in a course of psychotherapy, it is important that stability, security, and empathy are present.[57]

Finally, although there are main "guidelines" that are similar for different therapies, patients suffering from PTSD may differ regarding the number, intensity, type, and duration of traumatic events experienced, and individual variables and coping strategies may also change from subject to subject. Therefore, assessment strategies, criteria for diagnostic decisions, and different approaches to the treatment of this disorder should be chosen according to the specificity of each case; for example, it is not advisable to approach "*combat-related PTSD*" and "*civilian-related PTSD*" in the same way.[58]

> *How was I to find the words that would pass from me to him? How did I bridge the agitation the calm, the light and the dark, how did he blow the sewer, the overflowing river of decaying matter, the malignant current of fear that separated us, me from him, me from others?*
>
> *Cardinal M. 1975, 2004, p. 7*[59]

[57] For further discussion, see the bibliography: Kernberg O. (2014) *Preface* in Mucci C. *Trauma e perdono*, Raffaello Cortina Publisher, Milan.

[58] For further discussion, see bibliography: Penk W.E. (1989) *Posttraumatic stress disorder. selected issues*, Journal of Clinical Psychology, XLV; 5, 688–832.

[59] For further study, see bibliography: Cardinal M. (2004) Le parole per dirlo, Feltrinelli, Milan, original edition 1975.

CHAPTER 3

Deterior Tunnel

Abstract This chapter explores the previously introduced issue of negative attachment; it highlights that depression is often accompanied by increased irritability and anger, which may play a role in the origin and maintenance of the disorder. The emotional stages one may go through after a traumatic event are then described, as also some social implications regarding depression. Finally, the chapter highlights that depression can also be seen as a form of defense from an alienating and frustrating reality, in which the depressed person withdraws and abandons himself. It points out that depression can be influenced by irrational thinking styles concerning one's social relationships, and that the therapeutic relationship can help overcome these issues; the therapist can also help the patient recognize and narrate his or her emotional states, and overcome feelings of guilt and inadequacy.

Keywords Negative attachment • Emotions • Anger • Relationships • Irrational • Therapeutic relationship

© The Author(s), under exclusive license to Springer Nature Switzerland AG 2024

F. Irtelli, F. Gabrielli, *Contemporary Perspectives on Trauma and Resilience*, https://doi.org/10.1007/978-3-031-70793-3_3

Attachment to the Negative? Necrophilia?

Depression is the feeling of being dead while the body is still alive.
Bauman Z. 1991 p. 30[1]

Max was abandoned when he was three years old by his mother, an unstable woman who showed up over time only to ask her children for money to settle her own troubles and then disappeared again for long periods. He commented that the mother went to great lengths to prove herself an unreliable person. The young man suffered greatly as a child from this abandonment, and as an adult, he reported that he almost forgot Mom's existence, no longer responding to her messages. Paradoxically, once he became a man, he became inclined to constantly prefer relationships with very unstable and promiscuous women. Max arrives for psychotherapy, sent by the psychiatrist who hospitalized him, for severe depression that erupted after his last love failure.

As anticipated in Chap. 1, it often happens that when the individual has been victimized by someone, a part of his or her mind identifies with the executioner, and sometimes the person adopts the attitude of the executioner toward himself or herself, denying himself or herself the possibility of being well—for example, in the latter case, choosing relationships that always promise new drama and tragedy. In this regard, we recall that Fairbairn defined the so-called death instinct as a concept that refers to what was later called "depressive organization."[2] In this regard, Mucci asserts that the death instinct is learned from the living environment and is the result of relationships that, instead of being vital, become the bearers of death; in fact, according to the author, the death drive has an interpersonal characteristic, and we can see it in action in dependence on traumatizing relationships and encounters.[3]

In Chap. 1, we also recall that we have already addressed and explored the issue of negative attachment, theorized by Anzieu,[4] which can arise after traumatic experiences.

[1] For further discussion, see the bibliography: Fromm E. (1991) *Die Pathologie der Normalität. Zur Wissenschaft vom Menschen*, Weinheim, Beltz.

[2] For further discussion, see the bibliography: Fairbairn R.G. (1952) Endopsychic structures in terms of object-relationships. In An Object Relation Theory of the Personality. Basic Books, New York.

[3] For further study, see bibliography: Mucci C. (2014) *Trauma e perdono, una prospettiva intergenerazionale,* Raffaello Cortina Publisher, Milan.

[4] For further discussion, see the bibliography: Anzieu D. (2012) Créer-Détruire: Le travail psychique créateur, Dunod, Paris.

It is also useful at this point to propose a distinction between the tendency toward necrophilia theorized by Fromm[5] and the attachment to the negative theorized by Anzieu.[6]

Fromm says that a particularly difficult aspect to treat in psychotherapy is precisely necrophilia. What is it all about? The author specifies that basic necrophilia means what the vocabulary designates as a person's perverse desire to carnally conjoin with another person's corpse. The author specifies that such things are quite rare, although they do exist, but he speaks of necrophilia in a much broader sense, that of the love of death, the attraction to destruction[7]; it is the tendency to focus morbidly and insistently on macabre and deadly aspects of one's own life and the lives of others, with a certain subtle enjoyment. It is an attitude in which death, destruction, and rottenness exert a perverse attraction. Fromm brings as an example of necrophilia Adolf Hitler, further specifying that the necrophilic attitude is scarcely widespread, but those few true necrophiles may also succeed in inciting others to necrophilia (as in the case of Hitler). An episode is told of him that certainly appears credible, namely, that during the war, a soldier saw Hitler in a trance-like state staring at a now decomposing corpse. That soldier had to work hard to rouse Hitler from that state and drag him away. Fromm states that the true fulfillment for a truly necrophilic character such as Hitler's lies in total destruction. Fromm finally specifies that the anal character described by Freud represents a more diffuse and less pronounced form of what, in the malignant form, is the necrophilic character. The anal character is attracted to feces and dirt, and in its malignant form, the attraction turns to death and everything that is at odds with life.

Fromm states that any individual may feel drawn to death if he cannot develop his rational and affective powers, and if he cannot, then humans tend to develop a different form of relationality: that which destroys life, as in the case of Hitler.[8]

[5] For further discussion, see the bibliography: Fromm E. (1991) *Die Pathologie der Normalität. Zur Wissenschaft vom Menschen*, Weinheim, Beltz.

[6] For further discussion, see the bibliography: Anzieu D. (2012) Créer-Détruire: Le travail psychique créateur, Dunod, Paris.

[7] For further discussion, see the bibliography. Fromm E. (1991), *Die Pathologie der Normalität. Zur Wissenschaft vom Menschen*, Weinheim, Beltz; *Fromm E. (1971)* The Anatomy of Human Destructiveness, Holt, Rinehart & Winston, *New York*.

[8] For further discussion, see the bibliography: Fromm E. (1991), *Die Pathologie der Normalität. Zur Wissenschaft vom Menschen*, Weinheim, Beltz; *Erich Fromm (1971)* The Anatomy of Human Destructiveness, Holt, Rinehart & Winston, *New York*.

On the other hand, attachment to the negative, which can be intertwined with depressive dynamics, is obviously a different phenomenon from necrophilia; in fact, a commonly observed defense mechanism in depressed people is the turning of negative feelings[9] against one's own person. Attachment to the negative also involves a reiteration of dynamics that primarily harm one's own person, whereas necrophilia is the pleasure and love of destroying the world.[10]

The depressed person may therefore turn out to be attached to the negative because he or she has become accustomed to being sick over the course of his or her life, so being sick turns out to be something he or she knows and is, therefore, something consistent and reassuring even if it is a source of suffering.

In a state of depression, we can thus observe how blatant the tendency is to systematically turn the positive or neutral aspects of one's life into a very negative personal point of view and to think conversely that when one has a constructive experience, this does not matter. This dynamic certainly differs from necrophilia and can instead be hooked into the concept of cognitive distortion that we will address in a moment.

Disappointment, Sadness, or Depression?

In the days following the attack on the World Trade Center in New York City on September 11, 2001, an estimated nine thousand mental health specialists, including seven hundred psychiatrists, stepped in to provide psychological support to survivors, witnesses, and members of the public. A month later, a New York Academy of Medicine survey of a thousand people living on the south side of Manhattan highlighted a 7.5% rate of posttraumatic stress disorder and a 9.7% rate of depression.

Fassin D., 2011, p. 54[11]

We should specify that depression can arise for a wide variety of reasons, and when the cause is a specific event, it is precisely called "reactive

[9] For further study, see bibliography: Freud A. (1936) *The Ego and the Mechanisms Of Defense* in Works, Vol. 1: Writings 1922–1943, Boringhieri, Turin, 1985.

[10] For further discussion, see the bibliography: Fromm E. (1991), *Die Pathologie der Normalität. Zur Wissenschaft vom Menschen*, Weinheim, Beltz; *Erich Fromm (1971)* The Anatomy of Human Destructiveness,Holt, Rinehart and Winston, *New York.*

[11] For further study, see the bibliography: Fassin D., Rechtman R. (2011) *The Empire of Trauma*, Birth of the Victim Condition, Meltemi, Milan.

depression"[12] (i.e., depression represents a reaction to a specific event); it is therefore correct to specify that after a trauma, such as may be, for example, an attack or an inauspicious diagnosis, a state of depression is considered a fairly common reaction,[13] although it is fair to remember once again that every reaction is subjective and determined by a great many variables and that not all traumas can be considered equal to each other. Clearly, for example, an HIV diagnosis[14] is a completely different eventuality from the shock of a love betrayal, but both events can be, in any case, the potential trigger for the onset of both a traumatic and a depressive experience.

One may then ask at this point what the difference is between going through a state of true depression or simply going through a state of sadness and disappointment. As early as the 1970s,[15] a clear difference between the two states was described: depression tends to immobilize the individual; he or she is then no longer able to call upon his or her own energy to carry out the usual daily activities;[16] the depressed person feels pervaded by a sense of hopelessness, and as long as he or she continues to be depressed, he or she generally sees no point in making any effort. The state of sadness and disappointment, on the other hand, brings sadness to the individual but does not immobilize him or her: the person's energy in this case is not severely impaired; in fact, if a person is sad, he or she rejoices at the prospect of experiencing something pleasant, the depressed person, on the other hand, generally does not react positively to the prospect of finding pleasure and enjoyment, and often the depressed person

[12] For more details, see the bibliography: American Psychiatric Association, DSM-5 Task Force. (2013). Diagnostic and Statistical Manual of Mental Disorders: DSM-5™ (5th ed.). American Psychiatric Publishing, Inc, Washington DC, it. Trad. (2014) Raffaello Cortina Editore, Milan.

[13] For further discussion, see the bibliography: Ryul J. Kim Y., Yun H., Han D., Choi N. (2016), Trauma, Depression, and Resilience among Women Living with HIV/AIDS in Kenya, International Journal of Psychology and Behavioral Sciences 6(2): 76–81 DOI: https://doi.org/10.5923/j.ijpbs.20160602.07.

[14] For further discussion, see the bibliography: Ryul J. Kim Y., Yun H., Han D., Choi N. (2016), Trauma, Depression, and Resilience among Women Living with HIV/AIDS in Kenya, International Journal of Psychology and Behavioral Sciences 6(2): 76–81 DOI: https://doi.org/10.5923/j.ijpbs.20160602.07.

[15] For further study, see the bibliography: Lowen A. (1972) Depression and the I Body, Astrolabio Ubaldini, Rome.

[16] For further study, see bibliography: Lowen, A. (1972). La depressione e il corpo. La base biologica della fede e della realtà. Astrolabio Ubaldini Publisher, Rome.

lives in the past;[17] not infrequently in the depressed patient there is also the feeling of having been harmed (by betrayal, illness, or any negative event), which is what many people describe as the worst long-term aspect of their suffering.[18] In summary, depression can manifest itself with many different symptoms, but more generally, we can summarize that it frequently presents with

> *invincible sadness, lack of energy, anhedonia (inability to enjoy normal pleasures) and vegetative disorders (problems with eating, sleeping and self-regulation).*
> *McWilliams N., p. 252, 1999*[19]

Finally, remember that in the tunnel of the depression, in some cases,

> *If the relationship with reality produces suffering and pain, sleep is a way to erase it.*
> *Salvo A., 1994, p. 139*[20]

Anger and Depression

Nancy McWilliams states that a depressed person often experiences his or her state often with anger,[21] so more specifically, we can ask how to observe such a link between depression and anger.

In the description of the characteristics of major depressive episodes proposed by the "Diagnostic and Statistical Manual of Mental Disorders,"[22] it was precisely noted that increased irritability can also be manifested in

[17] For further study, see bibliography: Lowen, A. (1972). La depressione e il corpo. La base biologica della fede e della realtà. Astrolabio Ubaldini Publisher, Rome.

[18] For further discussion, see the bibliography: Williams R. ed. (2009) Trauma e relazioni, le prospettive scientifiche e cliniche contemporenee, Raffaello Cortina Publisher, Milan.

[19] For further study, see the bibliography: McWilliams N. (1999) *La diagnosi psicoanalitica*, Astrolabio publisher, Rome.

[20] For further study, see the bibliography: Salvo A. (1994) Depressione e sentimenti, l'incapacità di essere felici. Mondadori Publisher, Milan.

[21] For further study, see bibliography: McWilliams N. (1999) *La diagnosi psicoanalitica*, Astrolabio publisher, Rome.

[22] For more details, see the bibliography: American Psychiatric Association, DSM-5 Task Force (2013). Diagnostic and Statistical Manual. of Mental Disorders: DSM-5™ (5th ed.). American Psychiatric Publishing, Inc, Washington DC, it. Trad. (2014) Raffaello Cortina Editore, Milan.

this clinical picture, which is substantiated precisely by persistent anger, a tendency to respond to events with angry outbursts and to lash out at others, and a great sense of frustration in the face of trivial things.

In fact, Freud[23] highlighted the fundamental role of aggression (which is well intertwined with anger) in the genesis of depression.

Indeed, anger can be significant in accounting for some depressive aspects: it plays a role in the origin and maintenance of depression and can also cover an obstacle to change; this emotion is often generated by the perception of having suffered an unfair harm[24] (which may be, for example, an unexpected illness or betrayal).

In depressive disorder, there also appears to be a relationship between anger and the attempt to recover the lost good to reduce the effects of the loss. Bowlby,[25] consistent with this, observes how often the grieving person (especially when he or she is also depressed to some degree) shows a refusal to give in to the condition of having suffered a loss-harm.

Anger is brooded over and thus manifests itself on the sidelines, when the person suffers from his or her condition (thus generally showing a lowering of mood) and believes, more or less unconsciously, that he or she has the power to regain what he or she has lost: in short, he or she does not accept more or less consciously the loss suffered.

The dysfunctional offshoots of unprocessed anger, in addition to depression, can also include sleep disorders and various other physical and mental health problems.[26] In summary, this emotion can thus be both a constructive spur to action (e.g., in the case of the transformative drive of a revolutionary, who makes anger his or her mainstay, or of a subject confronted with a toxic relationship that needs to be modified, or closed), and it can represent a pathological drift, for example, in the case of unprocessed grief: in fact, it is not possible to act in such a case, trivially, by resurrecting the deceased.

[23] For further study, see the bibliography: Freud S. (1917) Lutto e melanconia. In Opere, vol. 11. Boringhieri, Turin 1976.

[24] For further study, see the bibliography: Barcaccia B., Mancini F. (2013) Teoria e clinica del perdono, Raffaello Cortina, Milan.

[25] For further study, see bibliography: Bowlby J. (1980) Attachment and Loss, Vol. 3: Loss, Sadness and Depression. London: Hogarth Press and Institute of Psychoanalysis Tr. It. Bollati Boringhieri, Turin, 2001.

[26] For further discussion, see the bibliography: Stoia-Caraballo R., et al. (2008) *Negative affect and anger rumination as mediators between forgiveness and sleep quality* in Journal of Behavioral Medicine, 31, 6 pp. 478–488.

Thus, a lack of acceptance and resignation for the harm suffered and latent anger are evident at the specific juncture of unprocessed grief. When this is processed more plausibly, there is instead a decrease in depression and anger itself, which broods in the background.

Let us now exemplify then the emotional stages concatenating anger and depression that one often goes through, in sequence, after an unfavorable and potentially traumatic event such as an inauspicious diagnosis:

1. **Denial** stage (the difficulty in becoming aware of the inauspicious event takes place).
2. **The anger** phase occurs when the person gains awareness of what has happened to them.
3. **Bargaining** stage (the sick person tries to enter into a symbolic agreement, sometimes with God, fate, or doctors; he or she seems to symbolically "barter" the remaining life time by setting himself or herself milestones).
4. **Depression** phase (which is manifested both by the losses suffered, such as physical autonomy, and by the losses to be suffered in the future).
5. **Acceptance** stage (stage that is not always reached by everyone).[27]

Suffering a trauma, such as a betrayal, can pave the way for a similar path of processing: there may at first be astonishment, disbelief, or difficulty in realizing what is happening. Anger then often arises spontaneously; later, the person tries to deploy a kind of *problem solving*, tries to process what has happened to him or her, and at this stage, the individual may also reach depression, intertwined precisely with anger.[28] In psychotherapy, recognizing these emotions, naming one's emotional experiences, and learning to be aware of them also increase the feelings that can be recognized and represented, thus enriching our life experience.[29] Anger is, yes, a spontaneous emotion, yet we must also keep in mind that it is not always possible to take action to change all or even part of the situation:

[27] For further study, see bibliography: Irtelli F. (2021) *On forgiveness, the human experience of rebirth*, La Bussola Edizioni, Genzano di Roma.

[28] For more details, see bibliography: note 27.

[29] For further study, see the bibliography: Federici S. (2017) La rabbia: un'emozione divina, in Paura Rabbia Stupore. Le emozioni e gli altri, Edizione: I, Capitolo 4, Il Margine. Editors: Zoja L., Virgili R., Nori P., Federici S., Petrosino S., Malatesta K., pp. 79–105.

acceptance of what has happened thus seems to be a healthy step after any inauspicious event, regardless of whether or not it is possible to act.

It should also be pointed out that the recognition of one's anger (the feeling of being angry and the permission each person can give oneself to be able to be angry) does not necessarily coincide with the balanced management of it (which is a later step in the process of awareness): it can be a stimulus to change for the better but also the deadly entry into the darkness of depression.[30]

We can therefore finally assert that anger is neither good nor bad in itself, but it represents a pathway through which we can learn to recognize our boundaries and who or what threatens them; the choice to act more or less effectively and constructively is a subsequent and not automatic step. The feeling of anger, however, in essence, also helps us understand what we would like to see change in our lives; then, the choice to enact change in a sensible and balanced way is up to anyone confronted with this later release.

> ***Anger says "repent": stop bothering me, do not harass me, do not betray me, do not rape me, do not hurt me, do not appropriate what is mine, do not take away my love.***
>
> *Federici S. 2017, p. 97*[31]

Root anger consists of the reaction of an organism aimed at repelling, or destroying, a harmful agent.[32] It occurs not infrequently when we perceive physical or psychological interference with our world and what we would like to do, be, or possess. It is basically an alarm system that sounds when something of our physical or psychic selves is violated: it is therefore an inkling that is often activated when a boundary is invaded. Recognizing anger certainly does not coincide with engaging in rash, impulsive, or destructive acts but may instead coincide with understanding more lucidly that something harms us and that something needs to be changed. Legitimizing the feeling of anger thus does not necessarily coincide with making it destructive conduct.

[30] For further study, see bibliography: Irtelli F. (2021) *On forgiveness, the human experience of rebirth*, La Bussola Edizioni, Genzano di Roma.

[31] For further study, see bibliography: Federici S. (2017) La rabbia: un'emozione divina, in Paura Rabbia Stupore. Le emozioni e gli altri, Edizione: I, Capitolo 4, Il Margine. Editors: Zoja L., Virgili R., Nori P., Federici S., Petrosino S., Malatesta K., pp. 79–105.

[32] For more details, see note 31.

Therefore, it makes no sense to never acknowledge a state of anger, which is a state that needs to be reworked, as does depression.

Depression in the Background of Society

Every depressive experience, to the extent that it expresses itself with this fatigue of living, with this loss, more or less extensive loss of initiative, with this subjective rebound of failure and checkmate, comes into implacable collision with the paradigms that today's society.

Ehrenberg A. 2010, p. 46[33]

Psychoanalysis since the beginning of its evolution, thanks to the contribution of Sigmund Freud, has opened a reflection on depression in the context of the elaboration of loss and mourning.[34] In fact, we must remember that many depressive episodes begin beyond the biological component as a consequence of a loss, which is not necessarily a bereavement or the loss of a loved one but can also be the loss of a role, a social position, an autonomy that is fundamental for an individual to maintain his or her psychic balance. In fact, the depressed patient often reports that his or her feeling ill depends on external causes that he or she feels cannot be changed and that have a major impact on his or her mood.[35]

We must remember that in the past, in society, the depressive state was mostly associated with the sin of sloth, the vice of laziness, only to be framed by modern medicine and clinical psychology first as a mental illness, and then, given the difficulties of finding a shared and biologically based etiopathogenesis, it was converted into a mental disorder classified in international psychodiagnostic manuals.[36] We must remember that this evolution took place through the 1970s, when depression became

[33] For further study, see the bibliography: Ehrenberg A. (2010) *The Fatigue of Being Self*, Depression and Society, Einaudi Editore, Turin.

[34] For further study, see the bibliography: Freud S. (1917) Lutto e melanconia. In Opere, vol. 11. Boringhieri, Turin 1976.

[35] For more details, see the bibliography: Zacchetti E. Castelnuovo G. (2021) Il trattamento della depressione tra illusioni e speranze, esperienze e interventi in psicologia clinica, Franco Angeli Publisher, Milan.

[36] For more details, see bibliography: note 35.

somewhat of a fashionable disease,[37] and then through the 1980s, when depression was contextualized as a chronic illness.[38]

Currently, however, the World Health Organization defines depression as one of today's major public health problems; in fact, the depressive state is now among the best-known conditions, often known by many people even from direct personal experience or from their own friends and family circles.[39]

A sentimental difficulty, a bereavement, an employment crisis, or a professional failure often generate transient states of sadness that, however, can sometimes escalate into a full-blown psychopathology and even become chronic.

The concauses of depression today often include not only single traumatic events but also, according to Zacchetti and Castelnuovo, the overall framework of contemporary society, which paradoxically encourages depression since the spread of technologies tends to lead to a poverty of relationships and isolation in the virtual space.[40]

Thus, the Western context is not an antidote for depression today; in fact, studies devoted to the social context—which have shown that there is no correlation today between happiness and wealth and technological progress[41]—are also long known, and it is well known that suicide rates are often high in countries where there is more prosperity and means to build contexts of happiness, which, however, clearly cannot be so easily constructed artificially.

We also quote in this regard the words of the well-known sociologist Bauman:

> *Rather, a social index that seems to grow spectacularly with affluence, at the same rate that was promised and predicted for increased subjective well-being, is that of crime: Of car and house thefts, drug trafficking, bribes and corruption*

[37] For further study, see the bibliography: Ehrenberg A. (2010) *The struggle to be oneself, depression and* society, Einaudi Editore, Turin.

[38] For more details, see note 37.

[39] For more details, see the bibliography: Zacchetti E. Castelnuovo G. (2021) Il trattamento della depressione tra illusioni e speranze, esperienze e interventi in psicologia clinica, Franco Angeli Publisher, Milan.

[40] For more details, see note 39.

[41] For further discussion, see the bibliography: Easterlin, R. A (2001). Income and Happiness: Toward a Unified Theory. The Economic Journal, 111(473), 465–48412345.

Easterlin R. A. (2003) "Inaugural article: Explaining happiness." In Proceedings of the National Academy of Sciences, 100, 1 pp. 176–183.

in business; of that uncomfortable and unpleasant feeling of uncertainty that is difficult to bear and even more difficult to live with constantly; of a widespread, ubiquitous but seemingly fluctuating, unspecified "environmental" uncertainty that is all the more annoying and exasperating for that reason.
Bauman, 2008, p. 5[42]

Finally, Fromm[43] states that those who are victims of depression are probably not so alienated or apathetic and out of touch with reality than are all other people, who nevertheless put up better defenses and adapt better to the social context, while Ehrenberg reminds us that the depressed person evidences just the opposite of the norms of socialization.[44]

The Illusions in Which Depression Is Rooted

Roberto was warmly invited to participate in psychotherapy interviews after an attempted suicide, and he arrived accompanied by several family members who were in turn concerned about the situation. Roberto, in the interviews, keeps repeating "my life sucks, no one truly cares about me" and comments on the presence of relatives, "they do not count; they just feel obligated to be here." It emerged in the interviews that several friends had shown up at his home to celebrate his birthday, and Roberto's comment was "they only showed up as a courtesy and anyway if they truly knew me they would not want anything to do with me."

Why does this kind of thinking take place?

Freud had already noted some irrational mechanisms enacted by patients during a depressive state: depressed people turn away from others and direct much of their negative affect toward themselves, hating themselves disproportionately to their actual shortcomings;[45] in fact, the depressive tendency often implies that the sufferer mistakenly attributes their successes only to the merits of others and failures exclusively to their

[42] For further study, see the bibliography: Bauman Z. (2008) The Art of Life. Cambridge: Polity, Cambridge.

[43] For further discussion, see the bibliography: Fromm E. (1991) *Die Pathologie der Normalität. Zur Wissenschaft vom Menschen*, Weinheim, Beltz.

[44] For further study, see the bibliography: Ehrenberg A. (2010) *The struggle to be oneself, depression and society*, Einaudi Editore, Turin.

[45] For further study, see bibliography: Freud S. (1917) *Mourning and Melancholia*, Works, vol. 8, Boringhieri, Turin 1976.

own personal limitations.[46] We should also specify that depressed people often complain about their own anger, indirection, vanity, and fear that they are inherently destructive.[47] In the wake of these dynamics, slowly and progressively, depression tends to invade every space of a person's relational life, crystallizing psychic and behavioral patterns over time, often leading to a perception of a distorted view of life, a distortion of the space of time that seems to flatten out and leave no hope for change.[48]

Not only in the psychoanalytic field has the typical irrationality of the depressed individual been noted. Indeed, in other fields, spontaneous unreasonable thoughts have been observed to correlate precisely with the state of depression, which was first defined by Beck and coworkers as cognitive distortions.[49] According to Beck's view, depressed patients exhibit the famous cognitive triad: they have a negative view of their world, a negative view of themselves, and a negative view of the future. These distorted views modify reality by making it grim and seemingly unchangeable in a vicious cycle that is always the same and tends to invade all aspects of the person's life.[50]

Burns[51] later expanded the list created by Beck regarding the irrational thinking styles typical of depressed people. In this regard, the cognitivist model considers depressive symptoms to be the expression of dysfunctional ways of evaluating various situations in life, since the depressed person perceives everything that happens to him or her as being wrapped in a negativity that he or she has constructed a priori and that, being in a depressed state, he or she no longer seems able to modify.

We can therefore briefly give some examples in this regard:

[46] For further study, see bibliography: McWilliams N. (1999) *La diagnosi psicoanalitica*, Astrolabio Publisher, Rome.

[47] For more details, see note 46.

[48] For more details, see the bibliography: Zacchetti E. Castelnuovo G. (2021) Il trattamento della depressione tra illusioni e speranze, esperienze e interventi in psicologia clinica, Franco Angeli Publisher, Milan.

[49] For further discussion, see the bibliography: Beck A. T., Rush A., Shaw B., Emery, G. (1979) *Cognitive therapy of depression*. Guilford, New York, NY, USA: Guilford; Dozois D. J. A., Beck A. T. (2008). *Cognitive schemas, beliefs and assumptions*. In K. S. Dobson & D. J. A. Dozois (Eds.), *Risk factors in depression* (pp. 121–143). Elsevier/Academic Press, Oxford, United Kingdom.

[50] For further study see the bibliography: Beck A. (1976) *Principles of Cognitive Therapy*, Astrolabe, Rome.

[51] For further study, see the bibliography: Burns D. D. (1980) *Feeling good: The new mood therapy*, Signet, New York, NY, USA.

1. *All-or-nothing thinking*, that is, seeing something as all white or all black without considering the full range of possible evaluations. This is the tendency to consider the situation in an extreme way and thus to have an irrationally categorical point of view. An example may be the clinical case of a girl who was competitively practicing her sport and one day lost a very important competition; after that episode, she was obsessed with the idea that she was a complete failure, fell into depression and wanted to quit her competitive career completely. "All black or all white" thinking is the basis of perfectionism, and this viewpoint often leads one to be obsessed and appalled by failure because one believes that in case it takes place, then one is completely worthless and inadequate, risking making irrational decisions.[52]
2. *Filtering* refers to focusing on negative information and devaluing positive information. For example, Diana invited a dozen friends over even though she was going through a period of mood deflection, she thought that hanging out with someone would be good for her; to set up the appetizer, she ordered at her own expense some pizzas to share and prepare some dishes, such as savory brioche. *All the friends are thankful for the buffet and consume the meal peacefully, but one guest, known to all to be a profiteer and an opportunist, turns to Diana in a brusque, rude, and aggressive manner and asks her to have some protein right away because the girl only bought carbohydrates. The other guests look at the exploiter with pity. Diana immediately offers him a can of tuna without comment, but from that day, she decides not to invite anyone to the house again to avoid such episodes of rudeness. It would have been more rational to decide instead to organize other social occasions with polite friends, selectively excluding only the profiteers such as the rude person who attacked her, to whom she could instead have lucidly and promptly responded, for example, "when you organize an aperitif at your own expense you will also buy protein, but I am not aware that you have ever offered one to anyone."*
3. *Overgeneralization*, that is, the assumption that the occurrence of a bad event means that further bad events will definitely occur. An example in this regard is the case of a guy who was cheated on by his partner after many months of dating and who was unable to

[52] It can be stated very trivially that such a viewpoint is unrealistic since absolutes almost always do not exist in normal everyday life, this viewpoint represents an unrealistic viewpoint.

overcome the crisis and who decided to leave the girl for good. Thereafter, he actively avoided any kind of sexual, sentimental, and emotional experience, fell into a deep depression and came to psychotherapy obsessed with the idea that any romance would end the same way and that, although he suffered greatly from loneliness, he would remain single forever to prevent disappointment. It may happen that, after an unpleasant episode, a person thinks that the same juncture can repeat itself repeatedly indefinitely. Such pessimism is unrealistic and arises from continuously generalizing an unpleasant episode from the past; more trivially, without this continuous generalization, a fact may be disturbing for a circumscribed period of time. Instead, by continuing to generalize, the boy came to the conclusion that since one girl had cheated on him, then all the other people he would later meet would systematically do so as well, following the irrational thought that "all girls are the same."

4. *Personalization* involves irrationally assuming that one is the cause of a negative event. In cases of major psychotic depression, for example, the individual may be truly convinced that he or she is the sole trigger for the outbreak of an international war conflict. It is important to address psychotic issues of this kind during a course of psychotherapy.

Depression and Relationships

We must emphasize the importance of the relational context both in the onset of depression and the importance of relationships in the treatment of the depressive state itself; in fact, it can be argued that irrational thinking styles precisely within one's social relationships can be particularly relevant in fomenting and maintaining depressive symptomatology.[53] For example, depressed individuals may irrationally assume, "no matter what," that others do not have a good opinion of them, and this mechanism is often based on the fact that the depressed patient thinks negative things

[53] For further discussion, see the bibliography: Evraire L. E., Dozois D. J. A. (2011) *An integrative model of excessive reassurance seeking and negative feedback seeking in the development and maintenance of depression. Clinical Psychology Review*, 31, 1291–1303; Hammen C. L., Shih J. (2014) *Depression and interpersonal processes.* In I. H. Gotlib & C. L. Hammen (Eds.), *Handbook of depression* (pp. 277–295). Guilford, New York, USA.

about himself and therefore irrationally believes that others have the same opinion: "if I think badly of myself inevitably others will too." In this way, people tend to isolate themselves and worsen their depressive state.

In turn, the therapeutic relationship for dealing with depression remains a cornerstone of treatment that can restore hope in critical situations.

An important aspect of the treatment relationship thus concerns how the therapist helps the patient not only recognize his or her emotional states (depression, anger, guilt, etc.) but also learn to place them in a narrative that connects past events and present elements in new and different ways.

Recounting important events of the past means trying to relive those emotions that can ultimately be brought to consciousness; in fact, it is crucial that in psychotherapy for depressive disorders, we can bring the patient to first accept and then overcome the sense of guilt and inadequacy that depression generally activates.

The recriminatory and complaining thoughts of the depressed patient may also be a way of expressing his or her suffering and attempting to draw attention and help into his or her social context, but generally, the complaints tend to annoy those who live close to the patient, leading the person to be labeled a complainer and often to enter a vicious and unproductive cycle that generally leads to no improvement.[54]

Moreover, the depressed person often merges with his or her disorder, and being depressed becomes a way of life, a way of being that one finds it hard to abandon, even for the secondary benefits that the illness may bring. In fact, a depressed person often tends to disengage from his or her commitments and assumes the role of a sick person who cannot take on work, relational, or family commitments in a stable and continuous way. It must also be specified upstream that people also tend to conceive of themselves in the role of victim because this can have advantages; for example, they may feel authorized not to take any initiative, and this they may also feel as a reassuring attitude.

The purpose of the psychotherapeutic relationship is to help depressed patients avoid this role, which is unconsciously assumed but often becomes one of the main obstacles to improvement.

[54] For more details, see the bibliography: Zacchetti E. Castelnuovo G. (2021) Il trattamento della depressione tra illusioni e speranze, esperienze e interventi in psicologia clinica, Franco Angeli Publisher, Milan.

The process defined as *resistance* describes the difficulty in abandoning the role assumed over time in one's relational system, even if, on the one hand, there is a sincere desire to seek help (psychotherapeutic and/or pharmacological), that is, to be able to change one's physical state.

Often, in depressed patients, there are two opposing and equally powerful forces at work: on the one hand, there is the desire for change and to leave a situation of discomfort, sadness, apathy, and fatigue that seem to take away the life energy that allows one to appreciate what existence has to offer; on the other hand, there is the unconscious fear of losing one's role aimed at seeking attention, of being at the center of the family members' interests even by taking on a complaining role even at the cost of being called whiny. In the latter context, family members can also often be defined by the patient as unable to perceive the suffering that the depressed person would like to bring to their attention.[55]

[55] For more details, see bibliography: note 54.

CHAPTER 4

Coping with Trauma and Crisis

Abstract This chapter explores stress and coping after a traumatic event, which can also be seen as a challenge; the importance of coping for adaptation and mental health, and for the development of resilience and social connectedness, social support was highlighted as a factor that can affect people's physical and mental health, especially after trauma or crisis. Some research showing that social support can reduce the risk of mortality from various illnesses, increase quality of life, and prevent problems such as depression was then explored. The importance of satisfying and supportive social relationships was then highlighted, and the topic of psychotherapy as a distinctive interpersonal relationship that offers tools for change was introduced. It was also highlighted how the patient's internal resources can be activated with the help of the therapist, and the search for meaning of crisis and suffering. Psychotherapy thus stands as an opportunity to process the past and open up to new perspectives. Among the various psychotherapeutic approaches is EMDR, which stands for Eye Movement Desensitization and Reprocessing.

Keywords Stress • Coping • Adaptation • Mental health • Resilience • Social support • EMDR

© The Author(s), under exclusive license to Springer Nature Switzerland AG 2024

F. Irtelli, F. Gabrielli, *Contemporary Perspectives on Trauma and Resilience*, https://doi.org/10.1007/978-3-031-70793-3_4

The Perception of Stress and Crisis

There is a crack in everything,
That is how the light gets in.
Cohen L., 1992[1]

The term "stress" was introduced to the psychological field by Hans Seyle; he was the first to use the term to describe a range of physical and psychological responses to adverse conditions or influences.

Originally, the syndrome defined as *just being sick*[2] covered the stereotypical response of an organism to a wide range of physical, biological, or chemical stimuli.

Later, in searching for a term to represent this response, Seyle used the word *stress*,[3] an English term meaning "pressure," which was introduced by analogy with engineering, where it is used to denote any force that is applied to a body to test its endurance qualities. In time, this term was then also employed to refer more specifically to a state of nonspecific stress in living matter, manifested by tangible morphological transformations in various organs, particularly in the endocrine glands that lie under the control of the pituitary gland.[4]

The term "stress," which describes the reaction by the organism, is distinguished from "stressor" (stressful event, or stressor), a term that describes the stimulus factors that cause the above reaction by the organism.

Stressors can include serious factors (e.g., severe trauma such as the death of a loved one or a serious illness), minor factors (minor facts of daily life), acute factors (accidents), and chronic factors (e.g., a very competitive work environment).

Seyle also distinguished between eustress (or good stress) and distress; they were originally included in the broader definition of stress but were immediately referred to as distinct from each other.

[1] Quote from the song *Anthem*, album *The Future*, 1992, Leonard Cohen.

[2] For further discussion, see bibliography: Selye H. (1936) *A Syndrome Produced by Different Nocuous Agents,* Nature, 138, 32.

[3] For further study, see the bibliography: Selye H. (1964) *From Dream to Discovery,* McGraw Hill, New York.

[4] For further discussion, see bibliography: Selye H. (1993) *History of the Stress Concept,* Handbook of Stress: Theoretical and Clinical Aspects.

Seyle asserted that stress is an inevitable consequence of living; however, distress appears when the demands made on the person (both in their psychological and physiological aspects) overwhelm the capacity and energy the person can and believes he or she can expend in maintaining homeostasis. The stimulus demand can then have a more or less welcome meaning.[5]

This idea has been well illustrated by Holmes and Rahe in their construction of the Social Readjustment Rating Scale:[6] all stress can be classified into eustress and distress; the latter is caused by a demand considered disproportionate in magnitude, while eustress is caused by a demand considered acceptable, which creates a moderate and not excessive level of tension that allows one to cope successfully with demands. This, however, is only one aspect of eustress.

The concept of an optimal level of stress comes from the studies of Yerkes and Dodson,[7] who explained how increasing stress is beneficial for performance as long as it is moderate, after which performance will deteriorate according to an inverted U-shaped diagram.[8]

To clarify the union of Yerkes and Dodson's theory and Seyle's theory, it must be explained that the nature of each stimulus is related to how each person interprets it and chooses to react to it.

It therefore depends on the individual whether a stress will be eustress or distress. Eustress is the primary result of a positive perception of a stressor, while distress is the result of a negative perception.

Classification thus depends on what the stressor represents to the individual and what value is placed on it.

Seyle suggested that learning to respond to stressful stimuli with positive emotions such as hope maximizes eustress and minimizes distress,

[5] For further discussion, see bibliography: Seyle H. (1987) *Stress Without Distress*, Transword, London.

[6] For further discussion, see the bibliography: Holmes T.H., Rahe R.H. (1967) *The Social Readjustment Rating Scale*, Journal of Psychosomatics Research, 11, 213–218.

[7] For further discussion, see bibliography: Yerkes R.M., Dodson J.D. (1908) *The Relation of Strength of Stimulus to Rapidity of Habit-formation*, Journal of Comparative Neurology and Psychology 18: 459–482.

[8] For further discussion, see the bibliography: Benson H., Allen R.L. (1980) *How Much Stress is Too Much*, Harvard Business Review, 58, 5: 86–92. Certo S.C. (2003) *Supervision: Concept of Skill Building*, 4th ed. McGraw Hill, New York.

while responding with negative emotions such as despair greatly increases distress.[9]

Mental distress may be the consequence of severe stress, but mental distress (such as PTSD) may itself be a source of stress, and reactions to distress per se are also always subjective. In this regard, we should point out that Lazarus and Folkman[10] have also hypothesized that the ability to cope with a disturbance per se is to a good extent determined by the meaning that the subject attaches to his or her experiences; thus, personal meaning would derive from an assessment of how damaged, threatened and challenged one feels by a certain experience, as well as an evaluation of the alternatives one identifies to alleviate the effects of the event.

Therefore, it is important to consider resilience and vulnerability in terms of both the subject's response to the trauma and the subject's ability to cope with his or her own reactions. We must emphasize that stress caused by a psychological disorder can elicit the same sense of helplessness and the same threat of disintegration experienced by trauma sufferers.

Finally, we can specify that in the perception of the stressor and the attribution of meaning to it, the characteristics of the individual also intervene: presenting an internal locus of control has quite different implications than an external locus of control.

By locus of control, we mean the way an individual believes that events in his or her life are produced by his or her own actions and behaviors (internal locus of control) or by external causes independent of his or her own will (internal locus of control). Internal locus of control correlates with self-efficacy, that is, the belief that one is able to control environmental challenges by taking adaptive action; in accordance with social cognitive theory, self-perceived efficacy strongly influences behavior and is positively associated with adaptation, and learning to cope with stress by viewing it as manageable is another key element in the development of resilience.[11]

[9] For further study, see the bibliography: Seyle H. (1987) *Stress Without Distress*, Transword, London.

[10] For further study, see the bibliography: Lazarus R.S, Folkman S. (1984) *Stress Appraisal and Coping*, Springer, New York.

[11] For further discussion, see the bibliography: Shonkoff J. P., Levitt P., Bunge, S. et al. (2015) *Supportive Relationships and Active Skill-Building Strengthen the Foundations of Resilience*. Working Paper No. 13. National Scientific Council on the Developing Child, Harvard University.

The key term here is "manageable," meaning that perceiving that a stress remains within an appropriate threshold can actually have the effect of strengthening resilience by maximizing positive stress that is helpful to patients.

We can also say that it is in a certain sense an *ecological* discourse, an anthropology declined in an immanent sense, from which we can take our starting point for an opening to a transcendence, to a surplus of meaning that is such only if it originates from and is rooted in the *flesh of the world.*

All the more so in today's anthropological contexts in which, partly as a result of ongoing pandemic events and wars, we have moved from an individualistic spirit that leads and retreats into ourselves, from a presumed sense of omnipotence and domination of nature to the traumatic realization that the nature we had claimed to bring back to our manipulative logic, has turned out to be of superior, ungovernable, unascertainable power.

In short, the stress discourse should perhaps be shifted from taking on the anthropological excesses of extreme performance individualism to instead a new human subject as a Spinozian *passive power*, a contingent, limited power within other powers, *primarily* that of nature.

Inserted at this level are the different ontologies of fragility and vulnerability: fragility as an ontological constituent of the human and vulnerability as its external exposure.

In other words, fragility refers to the uncertain regime of being inherent in human nature, the vulnerability to exposure to contextual, environmental, and social danger of the human's constitutive fragility.[12]

As can be understood, care must always keep this underlying anthropology in mind.

[12] For further study, see the bibliography: Vergani M. (2015) *Responsibility. Responding to oneself, responding to the other*, Raffaello Cortina, Milan; Nussbaum M.C. (1986) *The Fragility of Goodness: Luck and Ethics in Greek Tragedy and Philosophy*. New York: Cambridge University Press; Jonas H. (1984), *The Imperative of Responsibility: In Search of Ethics for the Technological Age*, trans. H. Jonas and D. Herr. Chicago: University of Chicago Press; Butler J. (2005) *Giving an Account of Oneself*, Fordham University Press: New York.

Coping

The same event, as already anticipated, can have different meanings for different individuals, and trivially, when faced with unequivocally stressful factors (i.e., which for most people represent trauma), different subjects react in different ways and with different outcomes.

It should also be specified that there is no direct relationship between the courage an individual may have in dealing with trauma and whether he or she then suffers from posttraumatic stress disorder; for example, in World War I, men who had developed shell shock were decorated to the same extent as other soldiers, and among the decorated individuals, there is an abundance of officers with posttraumatic stress disorder.[13]

Upstream, we can say that achieving optimal adaptation still requires that stress response strategies be active but also multiple, flexible, and calibrated to the specifics of the stressors or stressful events involved.

The stress response is thus modulated in two ways by the psychological characteristics of the person: at the stage of perceiving and processing stressors and at the stage of coping with these stressors.

The characteristics that intervene in this second level and modulate stress coping strategies are called coping skills, and the whole process of reacting to and coping with stress is referred to as *coping, a* term that literally means coping, holding one's own, and struggling successfully; it refers to all those mechanisms a person resorts to in order to cope with problems of various kinds to manage, reduce, or tolerate stress.

Since the 1960s, there has been a growing realization that while stress is an inevitable aspect of human health, coping makes a large difference in outcomes related to adaptation to stress.[14]

[13] For further study, see bibliography: Miller E. (1940) *Neuroses in War.* Macmillan, London; Williams R. ed. (2009) Trauma e relazioni, le prospettive scientifiche e cliniche contemporenee, Raffaello Cortina Publisher, Milan.

[14] For further discussion, see bibliography: Folkman S. (1997) *Positive Psychological States and Coping with Severe Stress,* Social Science Medicine 45: 1207–1221. Folkman S., Lazarus R.S., GruenR.J., De Longis A. (1986) *Appraisal, Coping, Health Status and Psychological Symptoms,* Journal of Personality and Social Psychology 50, 3: 571–579. Lazarus R.S., (1966) *Psychological Stress and The Coping Process* New York, McGraw Hill. Lazarus R.S, Folkman S. (1984) *Stress Appraisal and Coping* Springer, New York. Lazarus R.S. (1993) Coping *Theory and Research: Past, Present and Future* Psychosomatic Medicine, American Psychosomatic Society.

Mental health specialists working with trauma thus work to promote better coping and thus a healthier future not only for the patients themselves but also for those who live in contact with the patients.

To support the development of self-regulatory skills and the promotion of a stronger sense of an internal locus of control is to help people develop an expanded window of tolerance that offers greater adaptability—they are elements that inherently support greater resilience—the theme of Chap. 5.

We must point out, however, that the development of the above capacities takes time, and as clinicians, we must deeply understand the importance of these elements to pay attention to them.[15]

We should also point out that frequently, as soon as patients gain a greater sense of well-being, self-efficacy, and confidence, they will take a rather spontaneous interest in greater social connectedness, will thus have a broader sense of community and will have elements to sustain more social connections, a topic we will address in the next section.

Crisis and Social Support

These "resilience" factors can minimize the intensity of acute stress (...). One of these factors is the individual's ability to reconnect with his or her social networks after experiencing trauma.

Williams R, 2009 p. 241[16]

It is necessary to clarify upstream what is meant by social support: social support is a multidimensional construct[17] consisting of a set of enduring patterns of social relationships that can play a role in maintaining the physical and psychological integrity of an individual,[18] so it is a factor that can influence the course of life after trauma and crisis.

[15] For further discussion, see the bibliography: Shonkoff, J. P., Levitt, P., Bunge, S. et al. (2015) *Supportive Relationships and Active Skill-Building Strengthen the Foundations of Resilience.* Working Paper No. 13. National Scientific Council on the Developing Child, Harvard University.

[16] For further discussion, see bibliography: Williams R. ed. (2009) Trauma e relazioni, le prospettive scientifiche e cliniche contemporenee, Raffaello Cortina Publisher, Milan.

[17] For further discussion, see the bibliography: Bodenmann G. (1995) *A Systemic-transactional Conceptualization of Stress and Coping in Couples*, Swiss Journal of Psychology, 54: 34–49.

[18] For further discussion, see the bibliography: Trunzo J.J., Pinto B.M. (2003) *Social Support as a Mediator of Optimism and Distress in Breast Cancer Survivors* Journal of Consulting and Clinical Psychology, 71: 805–811.

It should be specified that with improved health status, on the one hand, the patient improves his or her social relations, but on the other hand, good social relations also help improve the individual's health.[19]

A person who is better off may also have more energy and resources to engage in social life, as does social support, which can help improve a person's health status; this dynamic has been known for decades. In fact, as early as 1979, Berkman published the results of a study on the connection between social relationships and mortality rates in cases of serious illness.[20] The researchers found that those who were less socially integrated had higher mortality rates.

This publication had a strong influence and paved the way for further research[21] confirming the connection between social support and better health. In these studies, social support was found to be a major factor in endocrine, cardiovascular, and immune functioning; disease hospitalization; and health maintenance.

In more detail, the evidence linking social support to illness was examined, and theoretical models highlighting the social, psychological, behavioral, and biological pathways potentially responsible for these links were presented.

The authors argue that people with satisfying and supportive relationships find it difficult to imagine not having such people in their lives, and they highlight how much research shows that relationships based on social

[19] For further discussion, see the bibliography: Shonkoff, J. P., Levitt, P., Bunge, S. et al. (2015). Supportive Relationships and Active Skill-Building Strengthen the Foundations of Resilience. Working Paper No. 13. National Scientific Council on the Developing Child, Harvard University. Uchino, B. N., Bowen, K., Kent de Gray, R., Mikel, J., Fisher, E. B. (2018) *Social Support and Physical Health: Models, Mechanisms, and* Opportunities. In Principles and Concepts of Behavioral Medicine. Springer.

[20] For further discussion, see bibliography: Berkman L.F., Glass T., Brisette I., Seeman T.E. (1979) *Social Networks, Host Resistance, and Mortality: A Nine-year Follow-up Study of Alameda Country Residents,* American Journal of Epidemiology 109:186–204.

[21] For further discussion, see the bibliography: Uchino B.N., Cacioppo J.T., Kiecolt-Glaser J.K. (1996) *The Relationship Between Social Support and Psychological Processes: A Review With Emphasis on Underlying Mechanisms and Implications for Health* Psychological Bulletin, 119: 488–531. Uchino B.N. (2004) *Social Support and Physical Health: Understanding the Health Consequences of Relationships* Yale University Press, New Haven, CT. Uchino B.N. (2006) *Social Support and Health: A Review of Psychological Processes Potentially Underlying Links to Disease Outcomes,* Journal of Behavioral Medicine, 29, 4: 377–386. Uchino B. N., Bowen K., Kent de Gray R., Mikel J., Fisher E. B. (2018) *Social Support and Physical Health: Models, Mechanisms, and Opportunities. In Principles and Concepts of Behavioral Medicine.* Springer.

support protect individuals from a multitude of mental health problems, ranging from mild depression to suicidal tendencies.

This research also focused on the less obvious possibility that a lack of supportive relationships puts an individual at risk of mortality from various diseases, ranging from cardiovascular disease to oncological and infectious diseases. It also appears that being habitually lonely fosters a sense of isolation and hopelessness that is heightened in the face of life challenges.

In contrast, the strength of social connections manifests itself in the joy, sense of acceptance, and resources we experience as part of our relationships. This not only promotes positive mental health but can also influence longevity.

The evidence from this research suggests the role of social support in predicting lower mortality from both all causes and specific diseases, and these conclusions are based on more than two decades of research conducted in various parts of the world.[22]

The effects of social relationships on health are thus evident today, and many prospective studies show in summary that high mortality rates are consequential to social relationships that are poor in quantity or quality.

Over time, therefore, emphasis has been given to the study of the social environment, for example, even in the specific context of serious illness: it was revealed that the social environment promotes well-being and protects people from the deleterious effects of stressful events,[23] so there is clear evidence that social support not only improves quality of life but also reduces the risk of death.[24]

[22] For further discussion, see bibliography: Uchino B.N., Cacioppo J.T., Kiecolt-Glaser J.K. (1996) *The Relationship Between Social Support and Psychological Processes: A Review With Emphasis on Underlying Mechanisms and Implications for Health* Psychological Bulletin, 119: 488–531. Uchino B.N. (2004) *Social Support and Physical Health: Understanding the Health Consequences of Relationships* Yale University Press, New Haven, CT. Uchino B.N. (2006) *Social Support and Health: A Review of Psychological Processes Potentially Underlying Links to Disease Outcomes,* Journal of Behavioral Medicine, 29, 4: 377–386. Uchino B. N., Bowen K., Kent de Gray R., Mikel J., Fisher E. B. (2018) *Social Support and Physical Health: Models, Mechanisms, and Opportunities. In Principles and Concepts of Behavioral Medicine.* Springer.

[23] For further discussion, see the bibliography: Cohen S., Wills T.A. (1985) *Stress, Social Support, and the Buffering Hypothesis: A Critical Review,* Psychological Bulletin 98: 310–357.

[24] For further study, see the bibliography: Kaptein A.D., Weinman J. (2004) *Health Psychology: Some Introductory Remarks,* in Kaptein A.D., Weinman J. (eds.), *Health Psychology,* Blackwell Publishing, Malden.

Psychotherapy and Psychiatry in Coping with Crisis

Psychotherapy is a very special interpersonal relationship between a patient and a clinician, a relationship that differs from any other relationship: the psychotherapy session becomes, for many patients, a unique moment where they can tell their deepest emotions without being judged, where they can be understood.

Cionini points out that the relationship in psychotherapy is profoundly different from that in the medical field: there is no drug to be administered that automatically induces improvement of the disorder, but a supply of tools, including the relationship with the therapist itself, that can lead one to walk one's own path toward change.[25]

This author further specifies that every psychotherapy session shares at least four fundamental characteristics: (1) a wholly special interpersonal relationship between patient and therapist involving an alliance for the exclusive benefit of the patient; (2) a specific place, the setting within which this relationship takes place, a safe place in which everything that takes place is confidential and distinct from the rest of normal interpersonal activities and relationships; (3) the therapist's offering of new perspectives, new ways of seeing or doing things different from the usual ones and able to make sense of confused and undefined feelings; and (4) a set of procedures and techniques that specify the therapist's way of operating.[26]

The appeal of this form of treatment lies precisely in activating the processes of change, as taught by the famous psychiatrist and psychotherapist Milton Erickson: it involves the activation of those resources that are always present in each of us but are completely paralyzed, for example, when the symptoms of depression begin to run rampant.[27]

Victor Frankl further specified that a fundamental aspect to which every process of treatment, every psychotherapy beyond the techniques used of the model of reference on which it is based, should strive, and that is the search for a meaning of the crisis for one's life; in fact, this author elaborated during his lifetime a fundamental thought: beyond the fact that a man places himself in a religious view, the search for meaning must become a fundamental goal for life, and the alternative to this search is falling into

[25] For further study, see the bibliography: Cionini L. (2013) Modeli di psicoterapia. Carocci, Rome.

[26] For more details, see bibliography: Note 25.

[27] For further study, see the bibliography: Erickson M. (1980) *My voice will accompany you*, Astrolabio, Rome. Erickson M. (1984) *Works volume I–volume IV*, Astrolabio, Rome.

a state of emptiness and meaninglessness, which becomes the basis for the development of depression.[28]

Meaning, according to Frankl, is also included in suffering; in fact, he states that if life has meaning in itself, then suffering must also have meaning. Suffering in some way is part of life—just like fate and death. Only with misery and death is human existence complete. From the way in which a man accepts his inescapable destiny, and with this destiny, all the suffering inflicted on him, arises infinite possibilities for ascribing meaning to life, even in the most difficult moments, down to the last act of existence.[29]

Although at an early stage, acceptance of the suffering condition may be helpful, a turnaround is then needed to avoid getting stuck on the memory of the past and brooding excessively.

The past can be processed in psychotherapy, but a key aspect is to bring the patient to feel and see himself or herself in a new perspective: the exit from the tunnel of depression symbolically represents a return to life, to that psychic energy that allows us to go beyond the emptiness, that construction of meaning that makes our lives worth living.

For example, depression is based on emptiness, monotony, the perception that there is nothing so important worth living for, and the therapist alone cannot give meaning to the patient's life: meaning cannot be given but must be found in joint work with great respect for each patient's autonomy.[30]

During a crisis, the person experiences situations perceived as unchangeable, and the ability to accept them in a dignified way, seeking meaning in them, becomes a fundamental commitment to any course of treatment.

[28] For further study, see the bibliography: Frankl, V. E., Batthyány, A. (Ed.) (2010) The feeling of meaninglessness: A challenge to psychotherapy and philosophy. (D. Hallowell, Trans.). Marquette University Press, Milwaukee.; Frankl V. E. (1975) The Unconscious God: Psychotherapy and Theology. New York: Simon & Schuster; Frankl, V. E., Bruzzone, D. (ed.), & Fizzotti, E. (ed.). (2005). La sfida del significato. Analisi esistenziale e ricerca di senso. Trento: Erickson.

[29] For further discussion, see the bibliography: Frankl, V. E. (1946). Ein Psychologe erlebt das Konzentrationslager. Verlag für Jugend und Volk, Vienna, tr. it. Frankl V.E. (2005), *Uno psicologo nei lager*, tr. it. Edizioni Ares, Milan.

[30] For further discussion, see bibliography: Frankl V. (1984) Man's search for meaning. Simon & Schuster, New York.

Additionally, naming one's emotional experiences, learning to be aware of them, also increases the feelings that can be recognized and represented, thus enriching our life experience.[31]

It can be considered at this point that emotional awareness of this entire affective landscape is, however, a luxury that not everyone allows themselves, and psychotherapy is also aimed at achieving this awareness.

This is a very important aspect because tuning to our full range of emotions and feelings can enable us to have a deeper and richer experience of every facet of life. According to Rogers, if we censor/remove some experiences because we consider them uncomfortable and disturbing, we lower the threshold for all others, also denying ourselves access to knowledge of our own nature.

If, on the other hand, we allow ourselves to be comfortable with the entire emotional and feeling sphere, positive feelings can emerge even more strongly (according to this author, it is as if, metaphorically, allowing ourselves to feel pain also allows us to experience more intense joy).[32]

Moreover, exploring emotions allows us to sift through their connections to our relationship with our neighbor: emotion is in fact a signifying phenomenon that also indicates to us the quality of a relationship and our feelings toward a person; therefore, emotions should also be read as experiences of social relationships.[33]

Finally, we specify that to cope with a crisis, such as a depressive episode, medication has similar effects to psychotherapy, and the dropout rates of the two approaches are similar, but the side effects of medication are greater than those of psychotherapy, and the relapse rates are also higher.[34]

[31] For further discussion, see the bibliography: Federici S. (2017) La rabbia: un'emozione divina, in Paura Rabbia Stupore. Le emozioni e gli altri, Edizione: I, Capitolo 4, Il Margine. Editors: Zoja L., Virgili R., Nori P., Federici S., Petrosino S., Malatesta K., pp. 79–105.

[32] For further study, see the bibliography: Irtelli F. (2021) *Sul perdono. L'esperienza umana della rinascita*, La Bussola Publisher, Genzano di Rome; Rogers C. R. (1942) *Counseling and Psychotherapy: Newer Concepts in Practice*. Boston: Houghton Mifflin; Rogers, C. (1951). Client-Centered Therapy: Its Current Practice, Implications and Theory. La Meridiana, Molfetta; Rogers C. (1961) On Becoming a Person, little, Brown Book Group, London.

[33] For further study, see the bibliography: F. Irtelli (2021) *On forgiveness. The human experience of rebirth*, La Bussola edizioni, Genzano di Roma.

[34] For further discussion, see the bibliography: Qaseem A., Barry M.J., Kansagara D. (2016) Nonpharmacologic Versus Pharmacologic Treatment of Adult Patients With Major Depressive Disorder: a Clinical Practice Guideline From the American College of Physicians, Ann Intern Med 164 (5): 350–359.

It must be remembered upstream, however, that for most psychopathologies, the scientific community has now shifted the debate from the search for the best treatment between psychology and psychotropic drugs, in a logic of opposition, to a logic of integration of both approaches, on the assumption that both treatment philosophies have nonetheless scientifically demonstrated their usefulness.[35]

Indeed, living systems are extremely complex, consequently requiring complex interventions in which biographical identities, epistemological arrangements, and structures of individual disciplines blur.

In this regard, Ceruti writes that the term coopetition was coined precisely to express this changing reality, an ecology in which identities blur and overlap but do not blur, in which everyone depends on everyone and in which everyone nonetheless continues to play his or her own game, in which global survival imperatives are created that constrain local survival imperatives.[36]

The Use of EMDR for Dealing with Trauma and Crisis

EMDR, which stands for Eye Movement Desensitization and Reprocessing, is among the various psychotherapeutic approaches.

This therapeutic approach involves desensitization and reprocessing of traumatic memories through particular eye movements; this is an important acquisition among interventions to cope with the consequences of trauma (both PTSD, depression-related conditions and anxiety more generally).[37]

[35] For further discussion, see bibliography: Angermeyer M. C., van der Auwera S., Carta M.G., Schomerus G. (2017) Public attitudes toward Psychiatry and psychiatric treatment at the beginning of the 21st century: a systematic review and meta-analysis of population surveys, World Psychiatry, 16 (1):50–61.

[36] For further study, see the bibliography: Ceruti M. (2018) *Il tempo della complessità*, Raffaello Cortina, Milan.

[37] For more details, see the bibliography: Yunitri N., Kao C. C., Chu H., Voss J., Chiu H. L., Liu D., Shen S. T. H., Chang P. C., Kang X. L., Chou K. R. (2020). *The effectiveness of eye movement desensitization and reprocessing toward anxiety disorder: A meta-analysis of randomized controlled trials.* Journal of Psychiatric Research, 123, 102–113. Yan, S., Shan, Y., Zhong, S., Miao, H., Luo, Y., Ran, H., Jia, Y. (2021). *The Effectiveness of Eye Movement Desensitization and Reprocessing Toward Adults With Major Depressive Disorder: A Meta-Analysis of Randomized Controlled Trials.* Frontiers in Psychiatry, 12. Scelles, C., Bulnes, L. C., et al. (2021) *EMDR as Treatment Option for Conditions Other Than PTSD: A Systematic Review*. Frontiers in Psychology, 12.

Rather than being the result of a specific theoretical perspective, it arose from an accidental observation: in 1987, during a walk in a forest, Francine Shapiro noticed how certain rhythmic movements of her eyes (from right to left) were associated with a reduction in the perception of discomfort related to traumatic memories. Thus, the link between rhythmic eye movements and reprocessing and desensitization to trauma was discovered several years ago.[38]

In fact, it has been known for years that this treatment is rapid and effective for the treatment of various types of trauma-related discomfort, which is why several scholars are interested in it.[39]

It is an integrative psychotherapeutic approach, distinguished by eight phases, that combines aspects of different orientations of psychotherapy and is used to address traumatic experiences that contribute to clinical problems (such as depression).

It is guided by an adaptive information processing model and is compatible with various contemporary psychotherapeutic paradigms.

In particular, EMDR is aimed at the reprocessing of information related to trauma, so whenever we speak of "trauma," we are referring to the psychic manifestations of a negative experience from which a disorganization and deregulation of the person's biological system results.

Thus, trauma refers to a physical reaction, a wound caused by a traumatic factor (called a stressor) that involves an intolerable and distressing emotional impact.

According to the adaptive information processing model, the role of mnemonic networks is crucial in determining the development of clinical

[38] For further discussion, see the bibliography: Shapiro F. (1989) *Eye Movement Desensitization: a new treatment for posttraumatic stress disorder*, Journal of Behavior Therapy and Experimental Psychiatry, 20, 211–217; Edna B.F., Keane T.M., Friedman M. (2000) *Effective treatments for PTSD: practice guidelines from the International Society for Traumatic Stress Studies*, Guilford press, New York, London.

[39] For further discussion see bibliography: Van Der Kolk et al. (2007) *A Randomized Clinical Trial of Eye Movement Desensitization and Reprocessiong (EMDR), Flouxetine, and Pill Placebo in the Treatment of Posttraumatic Stress Disorder: Treatment Effects and Long-Term Manteniance*, Journal of Clinical Psychiatry 68: 37–46. Matthijssen, S. J. M. A., et al. (2020) *The current status of EMDR therapy, specific target areas, and goals for the future.* Journal of EMDR Practice and Research, 14 (4), 241–284.

symptoms or mental health. Indeed, mnemonic networks form the basis of perceptions, emotions, attitudes, and current behaviors.[40]

Adaptive mnemonic networks are thus the primary basis of learning, self-esteem, and other positive resources and behaviors; on the other hand, unprocessed recollection underlies pathology because it leads to the establishment of maladaptive mnemonic networks. Problems in the present are thus conceived as the result of "stuck," unprocessed past experiences and thus related to maladaptive mnemonic networks. The information processing system is further conceived as physical and similar to other physical systems physiologically directed toward health. Like wounds that are brought to close and heal, the information processing system brings disorders to an adaptive resolution; therefore, it must be stimulated and activated.

Disruption of the information processing system produces disturbing memories that are stored dysfunctionally. It is therefore important to facilitate the processing of the disturbing material so that the past memory is not relieved and reactivated in the present but rather experienced in a detached way. According to this approach, the process is also to learn.

Disruption of processing can be caused by high levels of disturbed emotions that may prevent adaptive processing of experiences. If processing does not occur, information remains enclosed in a neural network in its original state and is dysfunctionally elicited by various stimuli that resemble the initial memory, causing flashbacks and unpleasant emotions.

This factor becomes generalized over time and can be the basis of psychopathology, as we have seen in previous chapters.

This is because all images, sounds, and sensations related to the original moment are stored in the same way as they were experienced, as they are unprocessed, which is why some are constantly re-experienced at the psychological level: when perceptions of the present connect to mnemonic networks, various components of previously unprocessed memories (emotions, physical sensations, thoughts/convictions) are re-experienced. Traumatic memories are also, at a minimum, partly dissociated from the

[40]For further discussion, see the bibliography: Fernandez I., Giovannozzi, G. (2012) *EMDR and adaptive information processing. Psychotherapy as stimulation of self-repair psychological processes.* Journal of Psychiatry, 47 (1), 1–4.

subject's general affective and semantic network and are represented in a form that leads to distortions in perceptions, feelings, and responses.[41]

In summary, trauma involves interference with the psychological and biological processes that normally promote adaptation to the memories of events.

Processing is seen as the creation of adaptive associations between networks of information stored in the brain, so processing is also learning. By facilitating processing, trauma is resolved. EMDR facilitates a process of processing that allows new and useful connections to be made.

The EMDR procedure is based on eye movements that alternately stimulate both cerebral hemispheres: the left cerebral hemisphere has an analytical, planning point of view and leads to cognitive processing; the right cerebral hemisphere is devoted to alertness in cases of danger and includes centers related to emotionality. The EMDR procedure activates the target memory, and through a self-regulating mechanism, it stimulates the adaptive information processing system: traumas are similar to "frozen experiences in the brain," and processing through stimulation of both hemispheres facilitates linkage with adaptive cognitions.

As a signal of ongoing processing, the components/manifestations of unprocessed memories (images, thoughts/sounds, emotions, physical sensations, beliefs) during EMDR change/transform toward an adaptive resolution. What is "useful" is stored and available as information for future experiences; what is no longer adaptive is discarded (e.g., physical sensations, irrational beliefs).

The EMRR aims to improve cognitive and affective well-being[42] and is applicable both to traumas that have posed a danger to one's own physical safety and to traumas that endangered someone close to us (accidents, amputations, witnessing a bereavement), that is, events that can then cause posttraumatic stress disorder—defined as "physical wounds," whether to trauma, such as abandonment, rejection, or bullying (defined as "soul wounds").

[41] For further discussion, see bibliography: Edna B.F., Keane T.M., Friedman M. (2000) *Effective treatments for PTSD: practice guidelines from the International Society for Traumatic Stress Studies*, Guilford press, New York, London. Hase, M. (2021). *The Structure of EMDR Therapy: A Guide for the Therapist.* Frontiers in Psychology, 12.

[42] For further discussion, see bibliography: Edna B.F., Keane T.M., Friedman M. (2000) *Effective treatments for PTSD: practice guidelines from the International Society for Traumatic Stress Studies*, Guilford press, New York, London. Hase, M. (2021). *The Structure of EMDR Therapy: A Guide for the Therapist.* Frontiers in Psychology, 12.

All of these negative events underlie dysfunctional beliefs and conceptions related to nonprocessing of the event.

EMDR therefore targets experiential contributions to dysfunction and health (traumatic memory).

The "node" or "target" is the traumatic memory designated as the target by the treatment, is a biologically stored experience in a mnemonic network and is usually the earliest recovered experience that laid the foundation for the patient's reported problem. Memories are considered dysfunctional because they are stored physiologically in a way that does not allow them to connect to any positive/adaptive network, thus causing PTSD depression and other mental health problems.

In summary, the procedure involves accessing dysfunctional memory that has become "frozen," stimulating the information processing system by keeping it dynamic, and shifting information toward adaptive solutions (leading to desensitization of emotional and physical disorders). The integration of mnemonic networks due to processing makes new acquisitions possible in the context of current life.

During the initial phase of careful clinical assessment, targets for reprocessing are identified; also, in line with therapies using the exposure technique, the patient's ability to withstand potentially high levels of disturbance factors is assessed. It is believed, in fact, that in EMDR, the disturbance factor can reach particularly high levels, and the physical emotions and sensations experienced at the time of the traumatic event can quickly become accessible to consciousness. Thus, in the first phase, the patient suitability is assessed, the reported issues and related experiences are identified, and a sequenced treatment plan for reprocessing is developed. Before a detailed assessment of particular traumatic memories is made, the preparation phase occurs in which the patient's therapeutic relationship and emotional safety are established, the procedure and effects of EMDR are explained, and the patient is asked to try eye movements. Finally, relaxation and guided imagery techniques are taught to the patient who will be used at the close of the session and by the patient between sessions. The patient's ability to maintain awareness between the past and present is then reinforced.

At this point, an assessment is made of traumatic memories that will be useful in carrying out reprocessing; a target memory in particular is selected, about which the need to obtain details and minute descriptions is not considered. The questions that are asked of the patient at this stage are intended only to assess his means of understanding the information and to understand what he feels in thinking about the 'event.' In the Assessment phase, an image representative of the target memory is then selected by the patient, and the baseline is measured based on the feelings elicited by the image. The patient must then identify a negative cognition (belief) that accompanies the image at this time; this is important: negative cognitions take the form of beliefs about oneself (e.g., thinking one is unworthy) or descriptions of past events (such as "I was terrified"). At this point, positive cognition is identified through the question "When you think about that image what would you like to believe about yourself right now?" The subject's feelings about positive cognition were recorded.[43]

He or she is then asked to match the image and the negative feeling and to identify and evaluate the accompanying emotions. Once these procedures are finished, the patient is ready to go through the different stages of the actual treatment.

The purpose of the first phase is, through sets of eye movements, to alternate between pause moments and breathing exercises to encourage the reprocessing of traumatic memories.

Changes in traumatic memories and images are facilitated by hypnotic traces, as they "suspend" early negative beliefs and lower the patient's conscious defenses and resistance. Patients may report a number of alterations during and after different sets of eye movements: any changes at the level of images, perceptions, or physical sensations associated with the target memory indicate that processing is taking place. Clinical data indicate that images can change in form and content: an image may become blurrier or wider, it may have additional content, it may be smaller or larger, it may move away or closer, or sometimes it may disappear completely. Sounds may change in quality or volume, or dialogs may change their content. Emotions may decrease in intensity but may also increase, and either way, this is interpreted as a sign of processing. Patients may also report a decrease in the intensity of physical sensations or a change in the location of bodily sensations. Then, the traumatic memory is subjected to desensitization to reprocessing.

[43] For further discussion, see the bibliography: Shapiro F. (1995) *Eye Movement Desensitization and Reprocessing (EMDR): basic principles, protocols, and procedures*, New York: Guilford Press. Shapiro F. (1999) *Eye Movement Desensitization and Reprocessing (EMDR) and the anxiety disorder: Clinical and research implications of an integrated psychotherapy treatment*, Journal of Anxiety Disorders 13, 35–67. Hase, M. (2021). *The Structure of EMDR Therapy: A Guide for the Therapist.* Frontiers in Psychology, 12.

At this point, associations with positive mnemonic networks are strengthened and increased, reinforcing positive cognition (belief) about traumatic memories. This phase ends when the subject no longer notices the presence of residual tension or unusual bodily sensations while holding the memory and positive cognition in mind: reprocessing of any residual physical/somatic manifestations of the memory takes place.[44]

The closing phase of EMDR is designed to help the patient end each session as calmly as possible since the reemergence of traumatic memories can cause strong emotions: ending with relaxation techniques is advisable. The patient is then made aware of what to expect between sessions since processing can also occur spontaneously, and he or she is asked to jot down in a journal any thoughts and memories that may emerge between sessions; techniques for maintaining self-control between sessions are also taught.

The last stage is to evaluate the effects of the treatment and possibly identify other associations that need to be targeted. In summary, at the end of treatment, negative memories change in content, and in the way they are presented, traumatic experiences are considered part of the past from a more suitable perspective.

Cognitive assessments of self also change, and more adaptive behaviors are enacted; instead, typical PTSD symptomatology is eliminated.

Regarding the efficacy of this treatment, it was found that when EMDR was compared with fluoxetine for the treatment of PTSD, EMDR was more effective, improving even after the end of therapy. With the drug, on the other hand, patients return to symptoms.[45]

[44] For further study, see bibliography: Shapiro F. (1995) *Eye Movement Desensitization and Reprocessing (EMDR): basic principles, protocols, and procedures*, New York: Guilford Press; Yule W. (2000) *Post-Traumatic Stress Disorder, aspetti clinici e terapia*, McGraw Hill, Milan.

Hase, M. (2021). *The Structure of EMDR Therapy: A Guide for the Therapist.* Frontiers in Psychology, 12.

[45] For further discussion, see bibliography: Van Der Kolk et al. (2007) *A Randomized Clinical Trial of Eye Movement Desensitization and Reprocessiong (EMDR), Fluoxetine, and Pill Placebo in the Treatment of Posttraumatic Stress Disorder: Treatment Effects and Long-Term Maintenance*, Journal of Clinical Psychiatry 68: 37–46.

The EMDR was declared decades ago as the treatment of choice for victims of terrorism[46] and for those with PTSD.[47]

It can therefore be considered an effective therapy with numerous application implications.

By leading to adaptive reprocessing of traumatic events, EMDR can also promote posttraumatic growth, a topic we will address in Chap. 5.[48]

[46] For further discussion, see the bibliography: Bleich A., Kolter M., Kultz I., et al. (2002) *Guidelines for the assessment and professional intervention with terrorist victims in the hospital and the community*. A position paper of the Israeli National Council for Mental Health, Jerusalem, Israel.

[47] For further discussion, see bibliography: Foa E.B., Keane T.M., Friedman M.J. (2000) *Effective treatments of PTSD: Practice Guidelines of the International Society for Traumatic Stress Studies*, New York, Guilford Press. Bradley R., Greene J., et al. (2005) *A Multidimensional meta-analysis of Psychotherapy for PTSD*, American Psychiatric Association, 16: 214–277, February.

[48] For further discussion, see the bibliography: Pierce, Z. P., Johnson, E. R., et al. (2023) *Therapeutic interventions impact brain function and promote posttraumatic growth in adults living with posttraumatic stress disorder: A systematic review and meta-analysis of functional magnetic resonance imaging studies*. Frontiers in Psychology, 14.

CHAPTER 5

The Universe Beyond Trauma Surviving

Abstract This chapter details how psychological health today cannot be conceived of as just the elimination of a problem, but the promotion of a development of the individual. It criticizes the traditional biomedical model, which involves the correction of the deficit, and proposes the bio-psychosocial model, which considers the complexity and individuality of each human being and adheres to the complexity paradigm, which requires thinking capable of overcoming determinism and simplification. Treatment today stands as but an offering of tools, including the relationship with the therapist, that can lead to change. Siegel's thesis that interpersonal relationships shape the mind and influence brain development is presented next, and the topic of reflective function as the ability to read the minds of others and oneself, and how this can be exercised and improved in psychotherapy, is introduced. Next, the concept of mentalization as the ability to make meaning of the past, present, and future is introduced, and how this can be inhibited by stressful or traumatic situations. The concept of integration is then introduced as the process that connects different states of mind, creating a sense of coherence and continuity over time, and how this can be assessed by the coherence of autobiographical narratives. The concept of posttraumatic growth as a positive psychological change following a traumatic event is also explored, and the concept of resilience as the ability to live and develop positively even in the presence of stress or adversity was explained. Personal and social factors that influence the likelihood of developing posttraumatic growth and resilience are then

© The Author(s), under exclusive license to Springer Nature Switzerland AG 2024

F. Irtelli, F. Gabrielli, *Contemporary Perspectives on Trauma and Resilience*, https://doi.org/10.1007/978-3-031-70793-3_5

described, such as hope, cognitive style, mental health, culture, and social network, and the types of changes that can occur in interpersonal relationships, self-perception, and philosophy of life following trauma are explored. Results of studies showing that trauma does not necessarily result in poor mental health are presented. Finally, the importance of relationships and connections in recovering health after trauma is highlighted, and the possibility of recreating psychological capacities damaged or distorted by trauma.

Keywords Complexity paradigm • Interpersonal relationships • Mentalization • Integration • Posttraumatic growth • Resilience

From the Perspective of Deficit Correction to the Turn of the Complexity Paradigm

In the psychological literature, we are accustomed to finding publications on pathology, discomfort, and problems that plague human beings and useful methods of intervening in these conditions of suffering; however, today, it is important to shift the focus from an idea of psychological health as merely the elimination of a problem to an idea of health understood as the promotion of a developmental trajectory of the individual: this change of perspective radically alters not only the conception of health and illness but also that of human beings, their traumas, and crises.[1]

For a long time, health conditions were defined on the basis of normative models that produced models of health consistent with the epistemology and mentality of past eras; however, it is relatively recent that that past approach has begun to be challenged, focusing today on the complexity and individuality of every human being, which, to be grasped, also requires an openness to complex thinking, that is, capable of overcoming the perspective of deficit correction and determinism that is part of the biomedical model, which is now outdated.[2]

It should be noted that in our day and age, we are in fact increasingly inspired by the complexity paradigm, as the traditional biomedical model, which involves deficit correction, has been superseded: this shift began in

[1] For further study, see the bibliography: Irtelli F. (2016) *Illuminarsi di Ben-essere*, Armando, Rome.

[2] For further study, see the bibliography: Irtelli F. (2016) *Illuminarsi di Ben-essere*, Armando, Rome.

the late 1970s, years in which Engel in the prestigious journal *Science*[3] declared that disease can no longer be fully explained as deviation from the norm of measurable variables; therefore, in the following decades, a new epistemology called "complexity" was born, according to which treatment can no longer be reduced to deficit correction alone, since upstream health must therefore be conceived as influenced by multiple factors, which in turn are modified by complex interactions between biological, psychological, and social variables.

The biopsychosocial model is thus presented not only as overcoming the simplifying view of deficit correction but also as a dynamic of increasing complexity in the relationship between various biological, psychological, and social levels.[4]

Thus, a process of epistemological and professional change has begun that involves not only psychologists but also other health professionals.[5]

In the past, the state of health has generally been regarded as a basic level from which to measure degrees of discrepancy (to be corrected); beginning in the 1950s, even the World Health Organization, moving beyond the concept of health as the absence of disease, defined health as a state of complete physical, mental, and social and environmental well-being.[6]

This definition has been a turning point in health and social policies in many countries, and by highlighting multiple dimensions, it has been oriented toward complexity: in short, treatment can no longer be represented as the correction of the deficit[7] but rather as an offering of tools, including the relationship with the therapist itself, that can lead one's way toward change.[8]

A health- and complexity-oriented orientation therefore does not mean to overlook in the slightest the fact that a person presents signs of trauma

[3] For further discussion, see the bibliography: Engel G.L. (1977) *The Need for a New Medical Model: a challenge for biomedicine Science*, 196:129–136.

[4] For further study, see the bibliography: Bertini M. (2012) *Psychology of Health*, Raffaello Cortina, Milan.

[5] For further study, see the bibliography: Bertini M. (2012) *Psychology of Health*, Raffaello Cortina, Milan.

[6] For more details, see the bibliography: World Health Organization (1948) *Costitution of the World Health organization*, New York.

[7] For further study, see the bibliography: Irtelli F. (2016) *Illuminarsi di Ben-essere*, Armando, Rome.

[8] For further study, see bibliography: Cionini L. (2013) Modeli di psicoterapia. Carocci, Rome.

and/or severe depression and/or other mental health problems but rather to ask how this person can afford to move toward a better state of health, necessarily referring to all aspects of the person, respecting the starting point from which some people seem to naturally face life head-on and with great energy, while others tend to pull back, to row against it, almost as if they want to implement self-sabotage.

Therefore, during crisis, every experience, whatever it may be, has its own meaning that must now be analyzed and understood, ***not with*** a view to correcting a deficit but to promoting the development of the human being. Therefore, every form of psychotherapy aims to activate the resources already present in the person and the capacities that seem to be deactivated and forgotten; thus, autonomy is promoted, the ability to develop an awareness of one's own mental states and thus to rediscover not only meaning in one's own and others' behavior but also a self-reflective capacity that includes past present and future.

Taking an example with regard to depressive malaise, for the sake of clarity, it is therefore necessary to emphasize that the patient in a course of psychotherapy can process his suffering as a part of himself and not as something to be removed, and treatment today, according to this new point of view, must therefore always be perceived as a process with the active participation of the subject.[9]

Psychotherapy can thus be seen as a means of promoting autonomy and awareness of one's mental states, enabling the individual to understand the meaning of his or her own state and behavior and to develop a self-reflective capacity that encompasses the past, present, and future; thus, the goal of psychotherapy cannot be just the absence of illness but the presence of well-being.[10]

> *In concrete terms, the moment of suffering can be a moment of momentum*
> *Irtelli F. (2016), p. 276*[11]

[9] For more details, see the bibliography: Zacchetti E. Castelnuovo G. (2021) Il trattamento della depressione tra illusioni e speranze, esperienze e interventi in psicologia clinica, Franco Angeli Publisher, Milan.

[10] For further discussion, see the bibliography: Irtelli F., Durbano F., Marchesi B. (2021) *The real self and the ideal self*, in Psychoanalysis, IntechOpen, London.

[11] For more details, see the bibliography: Irtelli, F. (2016) *Illuminarsi di Ben-essere*, Armando Editore. Rome.

Reflective Capacity

Daniel Siegel asserts that interpersonal relationships shape the mind, influencing the development of brain structures throughout our existence;[12] in fact, interpersonal relationships can also promote mental health through collaborative forms of communication (such as that which takes place in psychotherapy), which involves the ability to reflect on the importance of mental states and to tune in to others.

In this regard, we can point out that the specific reflexive function is considered a developmental acquisition that already enables the child to respond not only to the behavior of others but also to his or her conception of feelings, beliefs, hopes, expectations, plans, etc.

This ability already enables the infant metaphorically to read people's minds and make others' behavior meaningful and predictable; in any case, it is a skill that can be improved even in adulthood.

The reflexive function is made possible by a multiplicity of representational models regarding self and regarding neighbor, organized on the basis of previous experiences, and it should be specified that in a psychological journey with the patient, the exercise of the reflexive function is also proposed, thanks to which a shared sense of the subject's experience can arise, which can also become capable of overcoming the symptoms and discomfort experienced.

Specifically, the reflexive function, referred to by Peter Fonagy, indicates in summary the ability to access mentalization,[13] and he argues in this regard that the development of mentalization and consciousness enables the patient to make meaning of the past, to understand and organize the present, and to actively plan for the future;[14] in this regard, we can also recall that reflective functions are an essential feature, but we can speculate that unfortunately, when faced with particularly stressful

[12] For further discussion, see the bibliography: Siegel D. (2012) *The Developing Mind: How Relationships an d the Brain Interact to Shape who we are*, Guilford Press, New York.

[13] For further discussion, see the bibliography: Fonagy, P., Allison, E. (2012) *What is Mentalization? The Concept and its Foundations in Developmental Research and Social-Cognitive Neuroscience*. In N. Midgley & I. Vrouva (Eds.), Minding the child: Mentalization-based interventions with children, young people and their families (pp. 11–34).

[14] For further discussion, see the bibliography: Fonagy, P., Target, M. (1998). Mentalization and the Changing Aims of Child Psychoanalysis. In L. Aron & A. Harris (Eds.) (2005), Relational psychoanalysis: Innovation and expansion, vol. 2 (pp. 253–278). Analytic Press.

situations (such as traumas), the mind may respond with an inhibition of mentalizing abilities.[15]

Therefore, it is important for people to promote and restore their health.

The concept of integration, on the other hand, refers to the set of processes that functionally link different states of the mind, organizing the self across the past, present, and future, and creating a sense of coherence and continuity over time, and we should point out that an individual's integration abilities can be assessed by the coherence of his or her autobiographical narrative structures.

We must specify that narrative processes involve modes of information processing that are mediated by the two sides of the brain, and within each of the two hemispheres, these processes can be the result of integration mechanisms, and coherent narratives are created by interhemispheric integration processes.[16]

It should also be specified that one of the main features of the mind is its ability to connect and coordinate information at any given time and over time, so processes of various kinds are organized into a coherent set of activities; to define the functions on which this ability is based, the term integration is used, and this aspect can also be promoted in a psychological pathway.

In some cases, it may be that psychic distress, crisis, and depression are also manifested in their effects through somatization, so it makes sense here too to focus on mentalization, that is, learning to perceive the different psychic states that normally accompany the various events in life, whether pleasant or unpleasant, and this process of mentalization of emotional states could, however, have a controversial effect in the immediate term related to the fact that by decreasing those symptoms defined as psychosomatic, more specific and psychic symptoms such as, for example, depression, apathy, a sense of inferiority and guilt could appear; in this regard, we must specify that discomfort in all the forms in which it expresses itself reveals the need to be decoded, interpreted, and listened to by the caregiver, and it is essential, therefore, that the person achieve an awareness of his or her somatic and psychic discomfort gradually.[17]

[15] For further discussion, see the bibliography: Siegel D. (2012) *The Developing Mind: How Relationships an d the Brain Interact to Shape Who We Are*, Guilford Press, New York.

[16] For further discussion, see bibliography: Siegel D. (2012) *The Developing Mind: How Relationships an d the Brain Interact to Shape who we are*, Guilford Press, New York.

[17] For more details, see the bibliography: Zacchetti E. Castelnuovo G. (2021) Il trattamento della depressione tra illusioni e speranze, esperienze e interventi in psicologia clinica, Franco Angeli Publisher, Milan.

Treatment also involves giving meaning and order to the often confused experiences and feelings; in fact, what is recounted by the patient in the first sessions of psychotherapy tends to be chaotic,[18] and in summary, in a psychological journey, both the reflexive function, mentalization, and integration are promoted in this regard, promoting awareness and coherence in one's narratives and making in summary order out of chaos.

Posttraumatic Growth

A well-done analysis must lead to the death of a person and the rebirth of the same person provided with his or her own freedom.
M. Cardinal 1975, 2004 P. 267[19]

Trauma can have different effects on those who survive it, as it does not necessarily result in a sense of demoralization or a feeling of being harmed; in fact, the role of the memory of the traumatic experience can also become a source of motivation, and a determinant of human conduct is the subject of much attention in both the literature and art.[20]

In fact, posttraumatic growth can also occur, which is a fundamental concept related to that of resilience; posttraumatic growth was investigated decades ago following negative events,[21] and the term posttraumatic growth was introduced by Tedeschi, Park, and Calhoun[22] and defined as individuals' subjective experience of a positive psychological change resulting from a traumatic event.

[18] For more details, see the bibliography: Zacchetti E. Castelnuovo G. (2021) Il trattamento della depressione tra illusioni e speranze, esperienze e interventi in psicologia clinica, Franco Angeli Publisher, Milan.

[19] For further study, see bibliography: Cardinal M. (2004) Le parole per dirlo, Feltrinelli, Milan, original edition 1975.

[20] For further discussion, see bibliography: Williams R. ed. (2009) Trauma e relazioni, le prospettive scientifiche e cliniche contemporanee, Raffaello Cortina Publisher, Milan.

[21] For further discussion, see the bibliography: Cordova M. J., Cunningham, L. L. C. Carlson C. R., Andrykowski M. A. (2001) *Posttraumatic growth following breast cancer: A controlled comparison study.* Health Psychology 20, 176–185.

[22] For further discussion, see the bibliography: Tedeschi, R.G., Calhoun, L.G. (1996). *The posttraumatic growth inventory: measuring the positive legacy of trauma.* Journal of Traumatic Stress, *9*, 455–471; Tedeschi R.G., Park C.L., Calhoun L.G. (1998). Posttraumatic growth; Conceptual issues. In R.G. Tedeschi, C.L. Park L.G. Calhoun (eds.), *Posttraumatic growth: Positive changes in the aftermath of crisis* (pp. 1–22). Mahwah, NJ: Lawrence Erlbaum Associates, Publishers; Tedeschi, R.G., & Calhoun, L.G. (2004). Posttraumatic growth: Conceptual foundations and empirical evidence. *Psychological Inquiry, 15*, 1–18.

Instead, with the construct of *resilience*, we generally refer to a set of factors that define the ability to succeed in living and developing positively, in a socially acceptable way, even in the presence of a stressor or adverse circumstances that foreshadow a strong risk of negative outcomes.[23]

Resilience is intertwined with the ability to learn, to develop intimate relationships with others, to motivate oneself to achieve goals, to set aspirations, and to determine goals and understanding of oneself and others.

We can consider resilience both as a predictor of posttraumatic growth and as one of the outcomes related to it.

The term "posttraumatic" specifically refers to a transformation that results in a change in the individual with respect to his or her ability to resist and not be harmed by the traumatic event.

Using the metaphor of trauma as a psychological earthquake, Tedeschi and Calhoun emphasize that growth develops as a result of a traumatic event of seismic proportions, that is, one that is capable of destroying individuals' belief systems about themselves, others, and the world and increasing their abilities to deal with emotional distress.

It therefore turns out to be very important to accompany the individual in the adaptive reconstruction phase of belief systems, and the psychological pathway or emotionally engaging relationships can certainly be effective in this phase to promote the person's well-being.

According to the authors, the probability of growth development is influenced by:

Personal ***factors***:

(a) the level of hope and optimism: flexibility and openness to pain and difficulties;
(b) open and complex cognitive style: the ability to process stress at both the affective and intellectual levels and to tolerate ambiguity and uncertainty, extroversion, and openness to experience;
(c) the tendency to take functional and unconventional actions toward the traumatic event;
(d) pretrauma mental health.

[23] For further discussion, see the bibliography: Cyrulnik B. (2001) *Les vilains petits canards*, Paris, Odile Jacob.

Social *variables*:

(a) distal social factors, that is., the culture of the social group to which they belong;
(b) proximal social factors, such as the social network within which the individual is embedded and with which he or she interacts (family, friends, or significant others).

The types of changes cited by Tedeschi et al. (1998)[24] refer to three macro areas:

Interpersonal relationships, such as increased appreciation of friends and family members and increased feelings of compassion, empathy, and altruism for others experiencing similar situations.

Self-perception, such as a sense of greater resilience and strength, greater acceptance of one's limitations, greater awareness of one's fragility and vulnerability, and greater tendency to seek social support.

The philosophy of life includes a renewed appreciation for each new day, increased wisdom, a heightened sense of spirituality, and a reorganization of the hierarchy of priorities and life goals from the perspective of full awareness of human vulnerability and fragility.

Undoubtedly, traumatic events can enrich various areas of an individual's life if posttraumatic growth is achieved, and it has also been shown in very recent studies that a psychotherapy intervention can precisely promote these changes and thus well being.[25]

In this regard, we must also recall upstream the words of Frankl, who reminds us that pain, guilt, and death represent the "tragic triad" with which man is confronted and to which he tries to give, in his own existential journey, a meaning, redeeming in a transcendental way what life places in his path.

[24] For further discussion, see the bibliography: Tedeschi R.G., Park C.L., Calhoun L.G. (1998) *Posttraumatic growth; Conceptual issues.* In R.G. Tedeschi, C.L. Park, & L.G. Calhoun (Eds.), *Posttraumatic growth: Positive changes in the aftermath of crisis* (pp. 1–22). Mahwah, NJ: Lawrence Erlbaum Associates, Publishers. Tedeschi R.G., Calhoun, L.G. (2004) *Posttraumatic growth: Conceptual foundations and empirical evidence.* Psychological Inquiry, *15*, 1–18.

[25] For further discussion, see bibliography: Pierce, Z. P., Johnson, E. R., et al. (2023) *Therapeutic interventions impact brain function and promote posttraumatic growth in adults living with posttraumatic stress disorder: A systematic review and meta-analysis of functional magnetic resonance imaging studies.* Frontiers in Psychology, 14.

It is possible that this tragic triad can be approached through optimism, which can help turn suffering into growth on a human level, derive an opportunity for change and bring out of the transience of life an incentive to take responsibility for one's actions.[26]

Furthermore, the concept of "benefit finding" also indicates how difficulties can produce elements of evolution (Tedeschi, 2004; Bertini, 2012[27]) through a new representation of the critical event faced by the subject; according to this point of view, therefore, the subject is no longer seen as being healed but rather urged, as a person, to leverage his own resources and actively confront a physically or psychologically trying reality.

Finally, according to Victor Frank, our worst life experiences can also be a valuable opportunity for growth by allowing us to discover new perspectives, discoveries, and possibilities. According to this author, freedom, contentment, and healing result from the ability to choose our response to every event that life presents, being able to identify purpose and meaning in everything we go through, including suffering.

Freedom is a choice that can be renewed every day of one's life, and freedom is based on hope, which in turn is based on the knowledge that suffering even if intense is temporary.

Hope thus makes it possible to focus therefore on the present moment instead of focusing only on the past, and this helps us open the doors of mental prisons.

> *Marianne's neurologist had said that several of his patients who had never been artists suddenly discovered after severe brain trauma that they could draw or paint and do it truly well. In reconfigured disrupted neural pathways, many survivors discover that they possess gifts that they previously did not have or did not know they had.*
>
> *A wonderful way to remember that certain tragic events, even if they interrupt our life path, can be a stimulus for our self to come to light. They are tools that show us a new way of being, equipping us with a new vision.*
>
> *Eger E.E., 2021, p. 31*[28]

[26] For further discussion, see bibliography: Frankl V. (1984) *Man's search for meaning*. New York: Simon & Schuster.

[27] For further discussion, see the bibliography: Bertini, M. (2012) *Psychology of Health*, Raffaello Cortina, Milan; Tedeschi, R.G., & Calhoun, L.G. (2004). Posttraumatic growth: Conceptual foundations and empirical evidence. *Psychological Inquiry, 15*, 1–18.

[28] For further study, see the bibliography: Eger E. E. (2021) Il coraggio di rinascere. Lezioni di resilienza. Trad. by Lucia Corradini. Corbaccio, Milan.

Nonlinear Developmental Trajectories After Trauma

When Lance Armstrong completed the last leg of the Tour de France in front of a crowd of half a million people, it was more than just winning the world's most prestigious bicycle race. The moment represented the triumph of the motivation of the human spirit; it had the miraculous. Only 33 months earlier, no one would have thought that Armstrong could aspire to such a victory. It even seemed that he would never compete again; in fact, some time earlier, he had been diagnosed with testicular cancer that had already spread to his lungs and brain, with 12 foci and various lesions. Doctors had given him a 50% chance of survival. The treatments he had to undertake were terrible. He underwent surgeries and four rounds of chemotherapy a month apart, but he did not let it get him down. He endeavored to cycle 20 to 50 miles the day after each weekly chemotherapy session. Later, something unexpected happened: the cancer disappeared, stunning everyone. Armstrong resumed his career where he left off, training for now every day and participating in many bicycle races.

Feldman S., p. 303 2021[29]

The Grant Study, which followed the health status of a sample of Harvard University students in a longitudinal study that lasted until these people turned 65, revealed that there was no relationship between the frequency of posttraumatic stress disorder and variables that predicted poor mental health through other measurements.[30]

We can therefore consider that human developmental trajectories are not linear per se: trauma does not necessarily predict an impaired life.

Allen Frances[31] also states that people should have more faith in the healing power of time passing, the ability of natural recovery, social and family support, and psychotherapy and that they should instead stop passively relying on psychotropic drugs; in fact, a trauma, a crisis, does not in itself represent a condemnation.

[29] For further discussion, see the bibliography: Feldman R. S., Amoretti G., Ciceri M. R. (2021) Psicologia generale (4th edition) Connect, McGraw Hill Education, Milan, Italy.

[30] For further discussion, see bibliography: Lee K.A. et al. (1995) *A 50-year prospective study of the psychological seqelae of World War Combat.* In American Journal of Psychiatry, 152, pp. 516–522; Williams R. ed. (2009) Trauma e relazioni, le prospettive scientifiche e cliniche contemporanee, Raffaello Cortina Publisher, Milan.

[31] For further discussion, see the bibliography: Frances A. (2013) Saving Normal: An Insider's Revolt against Out-of-Control Psychiatric Diagnosis, DSM-5, Big Pharma, and the Medicalization of Ordinary Life. William Morrow & Co, New York.

We must also specify that there are three different aspects of the healing process of those affected by trauma: the first is the demand for relational recognition of the injury, that is, the demand that there be a listener of what happened; the second is the recognition of the perpetrator of the action he or she has suffered, which does not coincide with having an apology from the perpetrator and does not consist of actually forgiving the person in person (we specify that this point, however, is unfortunately not applicable in the case of major cause events such as an illness); finally, the person affected by the misfortune also demands that his or her words be recognized as true.

All of these elements can create an empowerment of the person, who begins to feel that he or she is regaining power as a subject, a movement of reconnection with others and a reconnection with social life therefore takes place, although the timing is always subjective and relative.

We also specify that while the central experiences of psychic trauma are often the subject's sense of deprivation of power and control over self and the destruction of his or her ties with others, it should be specified that healing, therefore, is based on the restoration of the survivor of power and control over self and the building of bonds,[32] Herman in fact asserts that healing can only take place in the context of relationships; it cannot come in isolation: healing therefore is also rooted in renewed connections with others.

Survivors can also recreate psychological faculties that have been damaged or distorted by traumatic experience, and these faculties include the fundamental capacities of trust, autonomy, initiative, competence, identity, and intimacy. Just as these capacities are originally formed in a relationship with other people, it makes sense that they would be similarly reformed in relationships with others[33] with their own timing that may vary from person to person.

[32] For further discussion, see the bibliography: Herman J.L. (1992) *Complex PTSD: a syndrome in survivors af prolonged and repente trauma,* Journal of Traumatic Stress, 5, 377–391.

[33] For further discussion, see bibliography: Herman J.L. (1992) *Complex PTSD: a syndrome in survivors af prolonged and repente trauma,* Journal of Traumatic Stress, 5, 377–391.

The Importance of Self-Perception and Self-Expression

Reframing one's experiences is certainly important for a person's health, and we must remember in this regard that language influences a person's experiences, for example, an experience for which a specific language does not have a corresponding word to represent it rarely comes to a person's awareness: language embodies a certain disposition toward life and can thus be defined as an expression of a certain way of experiencing life;[34] moreover, language, grammar, and words are indicative of the manner and perspective of our life experience, and they determine what kind of experiences can have access to our awareness (if there is no term for an experience in our language, it is difficult to become aware of this specific aspect);[35] therefore, the individual often cannot afford to become aware of thoughts and feelings that are incompatible with his cultural patterns (according to which he was raised) and is therefore unconsciously forced to remove them.

When reality reaches awareness (and is psychologically represented), it substantiates the set of perceptions that represent individual experiences; therefore, we must focus on the fact that human beings do not react to reality as it is but react to their own perception of reality itself, and this perception is subjective and relative: therefore, each person may develop a different perception of a specific situation and, in general, of the world around them, and this process is also based on a person's concept of himself; it is also the set of perceptions related to oneself, which influence the perception of the surrounding reality.

The self is, in fact, a configuration of conceptual, organized, and coherent perceptions of personal characteristics and is a very complex fundamental personality structure.

[34] For further discussion, see the bibliography: Irtelli F., Durbano F., Marchesi B. (2021) The real self and the ideal self, in Psychoanalysis, IntechOpen, London.

[35] For further discussion, see the bibliography: Irtelli F., Durbano F., Marchesi B. (2021) The real self and the ideal self, in Psychoanalysis, IntechOpen, London.

In summary, the term self refers to the whole person as a reality, including his or her body and psychic organization; in all cultures, self-esteem indicates how the person is performing in life (in the right way or not).[36]

According to Alfred Adler, children and adults with balanced and healthy personalities universally gain confidence and self-esteem whenever they are aware that they can achieve a goal: in short, the sense of inferiority is resolved when overcoming a new challenge;[37] thus, overcoming a traumatic event can therefore benefit the individual, and levels of self-esteem therefore play a crucial role in this process, precisely because they are signals of the effectiveness of the individual's actions.

Another factor that is beneficial to the health of the individual is self-expression, which is one of the basic needs of the human being, and in relationships with others, this need for various stages of the individual's life can be accommodated: when one engages in self-expression, one is trying to convey one's self-concept, and self-expression can also function as a powerful coping strategy when one is under stress, and it can also positively affect one's health: self-expression helps people meet their emotions and self, and even simple forms of self-expression, for example, talking about feelings caused by threatening events can help people overcome some of the physical and emotional costs of those events.[38]

[36] For further discussion, see the bibliography: Irtelli F., Durbano F., Marchesi B. (2021) The real self and the ideal self, in Psychoanalysis, IntechOpen, London.

[37] For further study, see bibliography: Adler A. (1927) *Understanding Human Nature*. New York: Greenberg.

[38] For further discussion, see bibliography: Smith ER, Mackie DM, (2004) Social Psychology, Zanichelli, Bologna; Irtelli F., Durbano F., Marchesi B. (2021) The real self and the ideal self, in Psychoanalysis, IntechOpen, London.

CHAPTER 6

The Universe Beyond Trauma

Abstract This chapter states that **surviving trauma** reveals what we would call **resilience** today. At the conclusion of this discussion, it is crucial to emphasize that the skills underlying resilience can be **strengthened at any age**, as **it is never too late to build resilience**. Therefore, we can say that **it is never too late to embark on a path of healing and evolution either**. Resilience is intertwined with the ability to learn, develop relationships with others, motivate oneself in achieving goals, set aspirations and have determination in pursuing those goals. All of these aspects can be fostered through a caring journey. According to **Fromm**, in the course of life, with its joys and sorrows, it is essential to discover one's **individuality,** understand true personal passions, inclinations and ideas, and define a **creative purpose** in life. This process can also result from **psychotherapy**. On the one hand, the **traumatic memory** is reprocessed in therapy within a safe and empathic space. On the other hand, it is important to remember what Fromm said about coping with life's challenges. One of the goals of psychic development is the ability to cope with insecurity and loneliness, which is an ongoing, painful, and difficult learning process for those who have experienced or know depressive feelings. As we have discussed in previous chapters, cultivating relationships is crucial for mental health, but it is equally important to appreciate **distance from others at times**, without seeing it as a condemnation. This, according to Fromm, represents an achievement. On the path of evolution and well-being, each constructive step can be metaphorically represented as

© The Author(s), under exclusive license to Springer Nature Switzerland AG 2024

F. Irtelli, F. Gabrielli, *Contemporary Perspectives on Trauma and Resilience*, https://doi.org/10.1007/978-3-031-70793-3_6

the abandonment or death of an earlier evolutionary stage. However, this abandonment does not imply a definitive loss. On the contrary, the previous stage is reworked and subsumed into a new evolutionary level. On the path to wellness, each step represents an opportunity for growth. This concept also applies to the treatment of trauma and crisis. Psychotherapy, with its various orientations, and psychopharmacology are both tools designed to address mental distress. Studies have shown similar results for both approaches, and dropout rates are comparable. Importantly, psychotherapy and psychopharmacology are no longer pitted against each other today, but a synergistic integration of both is sought, taking into account the individual needs of patients.

Keywords Skills • Resilience • Healing • Recovery • Evolution • Challenges • Well-being

Resilience After Trauma

However, torn from the very roots of my existence (...), one must
Create until the day dawns. Against despair, continue to
Create so that the world does not collapse.
It is the very position of depression
This elicits creativity.
Kaës R., 2012, p. 56[1]

Survival to trauma is what we call resilience today, and at the end of this discussion, it is important to point out that the skills underlying resilience can be reinforced at any age, precisely because it is never too late to build resilience,[2] so we can say that it is never too late to embark on a path of healing and evolve either: resilience is intertwined with the ability to learn, to develop relationships with others, to motivate oneself in achieving goals, to set aspirations, to have determination in achieving goals, or to understand oneself and others (and all of these aspects can be fostered through a care pathway).

[1] For further discussion, see the bibliography: Kaës, R. (2012), *Il Malêtre*, Dunod, Paris, translated in Italian (2013) *Il Malessere*, Borla, Rome.

[2] For further discussion, see the bibliography: Shonkoff, J. P., Levitt, P., Bunge, S. et al. (2015) *Supportive Relationships and Active Skill-Building Strengthen the Foundations of Resilience*. Working Paper No. 13. National Scientific Council on the Developing Child, Harvard University.

In this regard, according to Fromm, it is most important in the journey of life, with its joys and sorrows, to also discover one's individuality, understand our true passions, inclinations, and ideas, and set a creative purpose for ourselves in life,[3] and this too can be an outcome of psychotherapy.

On the one hand, it should be emphasized that traumatic memory in therapy is reprocessed within a safe and empathic space;[4] on the other hand, we also recall what Fromm stated[5] regarding the ability to cope with life challenges, namely, that one of the aims of psychic development is both the ability to endure insecurity and the ability to be alone, which represents an ongoing, painful, and difficult learning process for every subject, especially for those who have known or known depressive feelings.

As we have pointed out in previous chapters, it is certainly important for mental health to cultivate relationships, but it is also necessary to emphasize that it is sometimes equally important to be able to appreciate the distance that separates us from others and not to experience it as a condemnation: this, too, according to Fromm, represents an achievement that helps people overcome depressive experiences;[6] in fact, it should be remembered that a symbiotic union with one's neighbor and passivity *does not* correlate with health.[7]

Certainly, as human beings feel the need to be in a relationship with others and to compare ourselves with a social group, however, it is equally very important to also discover one's own autonomy, one's own opinions and values rather than always adhering to preestablished norms imposed by one's neighbor or by the culture of reference.[8]

[3] For further discussion, see the bibliography: Fromm E. (1971) *The Anatomy of Human Destructiveness,*Holt, Rinehart and Winston, *New York;* Fromm E. (1991) *Die Pathologie der Normalität. Zur Wissenschaft vom Menschen*, Weinheim, Beltz.

[4] For further discussion, see bibliography: Williams R. ed. (2009) Trauma e relazioni, le prospettive scientifiche e cliniche contemporanee, Raffaello Cortina Publisher, Milan.

[5] For further study, see bibliography: Fromm E. (1971) *The Anatomy of Human Destructiveness,*Holt, Rinehart and Winston, *New York*. Fromm E. (1991) *Die Pathologie der Normalität. Zur Wissenschaft vom Menschen*, Weinheim, Beltz.

[6] For further discussion, see the bibliography: Fromm E. (1971) *The Anatomy of Human Destructiveness,*Holt, Rinehart and Winston, *New York;* Fromm E. (1991) *Die Pathologie der Normalität. Zur Wissenschaft vom Menschen*, Weinheim, Beltz.

[7] For further discussion, see the bibliography: Cozzaglio, P. (2014) Psichiatria intersoggettiva. Dalla cura del soggetto al soggetto della cura. Franco Angeli Publisher, Milan.

[8] For further discussion, see the bibliography: Irtelli F., Durbano F., Marchesi B. (2021) *The real self and the ideal self,* in Psychoanalysis, IntechOpen, London.

Recall that we have described how feelings of discomfort, anger, and guilt are frequent after experiencing trauma, and Fromm[9] reminds us that these negative experiences are also precisely the driving force behind the manifestations of depression, and they cannot be removed but must be contained and processed in one's own experiences: the ability of patients to process and integrate their experiences is a goal of the relationship with the therapist, but this ability is not a gift from the therapist but is gained with the help of the psychotherapeutic relationship.

We also specify in this regard that the therapist alone cannot give meaning to the patient's life: meaning cannot be dropped from above but must be found in joint relational work, with great respect for the autonomy of each patient[10] in his or her individuality and specificity.

It should be emphasized then that human beings do not react to reality as it is but rather react to their own perception of reality itself; therefore, each person may develop a different perception of a specific situation and, in general, of the world around them, and this process is also based on a person's specific concept of himself or herself and his or her self-esteem, which is precisely the set of perceptions related to oneself that influence the perception of the surrounding reality.[11] We specify that when we refer to self-esteem, it is the ability to appreciate the value and importance of one's own person in the knowledge that one can rely on oneself and act responsibly toward others.

It is also important to specify that in the field of social psychology, one cannot fail to refer in this regard to *self-fulfilling prophecy*, a curious phenomenon that has been the subject of several studies and is now known to the entire scientific community:[12] the prediction and the predicted event

[9] For further discussion, see the bibliography: Fromm E. (1971) *The Anatomy of Human Destructiveness*,Holt, Rinehart and Winston, *New York;* Fromm E. (1991) *Die Pathologie der Normalität. Zur Wissenschaft vom Menschen*, Weinheim, Beltz.

[10] For more details, see the bibliography:Zacchetti E. Castelnuovo G. (2021) Il trattamento della depressione tra illusioni e speranze, esperienze e interventi in psicologia clinica, Franco Angeli Publisher, Milan.

[11] For further details, see the bibliography: Irtelli F., Durbano F., Marchesi B. (2021) *The real self and the ideal self*, in Psychoanalysis, IntechOpen, London.

[12] For further details, see bibliography: Darley J.M., Fazio R.H. (1980) *Expectancy confirmation processes arising in the social interaction sequence*, American Psycologist, 35, pp. 867–881; Harris M.J., Rosenthal R. (1985) *Mediation of interpersonal expectancy effect: 31 meta-analyses*, Psychological Bulletin, 97, pp. 363–386; Merton R. (1948) *The Self-fulfilling prophecy*, Antioch Review, 8, pp. 193–210; Smith E. R., Mackie D.M. (2004) *Social psychology*, Zanichelli, Bologna; Irtelli F. (2016) *Illuminarsi di Ben-essere*, Armando, Rome.

thus result in a circular relationship, according to which the prediction generates the event and the event verifies the prediction.

We can also define this phenomenon, in another way, as a process by which a person's expectations of a situation, or of an individual person, become reality as they prompt behaviors that can confirm them.

Numerous studies published in international scientific journals have confirmed this fact, screening it in various areas: affective, school, work, and friendship.[13]

Scientific research also provides evidence in this regard: subjective processing and attitudes have effects on health; in fact, it was found that men who, when they were in their early twenties, had explained negative events in a more defeatist manner experienced worse physical and mental health until they were sixty years old and beyond.[14]

Thus, we observe how an individual who perceives himself or herself as "constructive," that is, able to cope with the challenges affecting mental and physical health, is more likely to experience more constructive feelings and experiences in his or her innermost self and, in probabilistic terms, will experience positive development because he or she will be predisposed to these conditions at various levels.

Psychotherapy can therefore promote this constructive perspective on oneself because it must be remembered that trusting humans to give themselves a positive chance is therefore a harbinger of better adaptation.[15]

Therefore, we would like to remind you once again that

> *We can define it as a process by which a person's expectations of a situation, or of an individual person specifically, become reality, in that they prompt behaviors that can confirm them, and numerous studies, published in international scientific journals, have confirmed this by sifting through various domains: affective, friendship, school and work (...), but not only that subjective elabora-*

[13]For further discussion, see bibliography:For further discussion see bibliography: Darley J.M., Fazio R.H. (1980). *Expectancy confirmation processes arising in the social interaction sequence*, American Psychologist, 35, pp. 867–881; Harris M.J., Rosenthal R. (1985), *Mediation of interpersonal expectancy effect: 31 meta-analyses*, "Psychological Bulletin," 97, pp. 363–386; Merton R. (1948) *The Self-fulfilling prophecy*, Antioch Review, 8, pp. 193–210; Smith E. R., Mackie D. M. (2004) *Social Psychology*, Zanichelli, Bologna; Irtelli F (2016) *Illuminating Well-being*, Armando, Rome.

[14]For further discussion, see bibliography:Smith E. R., Mackie (2004) D. M., *Social Psychology*, Zanichelli, Bologna, p. 118.

[15]For further study, see the bibliography:Irtelli F. (2016) *Illuminarsi di Ben-essere*, Armando, Rome.

tions and attitudes also have effects on health men who, when they were in their early twenties, had explained negative events in a more defeatist way, experienced worse physical and mental health conditions up to sixty years and beyond.
Irtelli, 2016, p. 270[16]

Moving Beyond Trauma

Thus, psychoanalysis can help to traverse the crisis, both on the individual and social sides, by accompanying it in its tortuous passages: one then traverses the apocalypse through phases of apparent "nonsense," in which suffering and evil are actualized and sharpened before disappearing.
Irtelli F., 2019, p. 168[17]

The exit from the tunnel of trauma, crisis, and sometimes depression symbolically represents the return to life, to that psychic energy that allows the person to go beyond the emptiness, that construction of meaning that makes life worth living;[18] let us also remember that psychotherapy according to Victor Frankl's vision has the task of helping the person experiencing a situation that creates suffering to find with his or her abilities the best ways to change and restructure it, and where the person is experiencing situations perceived as unchangeable, then the ability to accept them in a dignified way, seeking meaning in them, becomes a fundamental commitment to any path of treatment: it is always possible, even in the most extreme situations, to give meaning to one's pain and from there begin new paths and create new opportunities for life.[19]

According to Frankl, the worst life experiences can also be an opportunity for growth by allowing us to discover new perspectives, breakthroughs, and possibilities.

Through a course of treatment, therefore, one can choose to live, to let go of one's past, leveraging one's freedom and strength, instead of always conceiving of oneself only in the role of a victim stuck in pain and the past.

[16] For further study, see the bibliography:Irtelli F. (2016) *Illuminarsi di Ben-essere*, Armando, Rome.

[17] For further study, see the bibliography: Irtelli F. (2019) Rosso smeraldo, l'epoca delle psicosi bianche, Armando Publisher, Rome.

[18] For more details, see the bibliography: Zacchetti E. Castelnuovo G. (2021) Il trattamento della depressione tra illusioni e speranze, esperienze e interventi in psicologia clinica, Franco Angeli Publisher, Milan.

[19] For further study, see the bibliography: Frankl V. (2005) *The challenge of meaning*, edited by Bruzzone D., Fizzotti E., Erickson, Trento.

According to this author, freedom, contentment, and healing are the result of our ability to choose our response to every event that life presents, being able to identify purpose and meaning in everything we go through, including suffering.

Freedom is a choice that can be renewed every day of one's life, and freedom is based on hope, which in turn is based on the realization that suffering even if intense is temporary; in fact, hope makes it possible to focus on the present moment instead of focusing only on the past, and this helps to open the doors of mental prisons.[20]

In summary, overcoming trauma and its effects is also embodied in learning to take care of oneself and learning to contain and integrate one's potentially devastating feelings, learning to be autonomous without denying one's need to cultivate affective investments, a need we all have, since we are relational beings:[21] the individual considered completely isolated is a pure abstraction.[22]

> *Indeed, we can say that unaccepted suffering creates a stalemate and thus results in rigidity in not going through it and in not accepting being in the true movement of life.*
>
> *Irtelli F., 2016, p. 256*[23]

We specified earlier that to cope with malaise, it is also important to develop mentalization and reflective functions.

To recapitulate, if in medicine healing is considered the result of a cure that is effective in eradicating the disease, and the cure is seen in this way as a kind of struggle to defend the body from the attacks of the disease, healing is thus conceived as a state in which the defense has been effective in fighting the enemy, and the effectiveness of the said combat is evaluated in medicine as the return to a state of integrity, that is, the integrity of the organ that withstood the attack of the disease, whereas in the psychological and psychiatric fields, the situation is different because the personality

[20] For further study, see the bibliography: Frankl V. (2005) *The challenge of meaning*, edited by Bruzzone D., Fizzotti E., Erickson, Trento.

[21] For further discussion, see bibliography: Siegel D. (2012) *The Developing Mind: How Relationships an d the Brain Interact to Shape who we are*, Guilford Press, New York.

[22] For further discussion, see the bibliography: Irtelli F., Durbano F., Marchesi B. (2021) *The real self and the ideal self*, in Psychoanalysis, IntechOpen, London.

[23] For further study, see the bibliography: Irtelli F. (2016) *Illuminarsi di Ben-essere*, Armando, Rome.

is always evolving and it may happen that at a certain moment in life this evolution comes to a halt,[24] for example, because of trauma, and we must remember that the concept of healing in the latter field is controversial; however, it should be specified that in medicine, treatment is aimed at healing and the term cure should be used when four conditions occur: (1) the restoration of structural, anatomopathological integrity; (2) the restoration of physiological functional integrity; (3) the restoration of subjective well-being; and (4) the absence of therapies to maintain the previous three conditions over time;[25] the same criteria can also be applied in the psychological and psychiatric.

In any case, upstream, healing in psychiatry and psychology can be a concrete reality and not an impossible dream, indicating that the term healing in this area is often paired precisely with the aforementioned term recovery, which indicates retaliation and recovery, the power and possibility that the patient has to challenge his or her crises, and the rediscovery of self and potential. In fact, according to this perspective, patients have unique unrepeatable identities, and human beings in their entirety who are experiencing a highly disruptive and interfering emotional state with their activities[26] and who are receiving curative interventions aimed at recovery and healing should help patients have a life richer in expectations, purposefulness of success and satisfaction and not just less burdened by symptoms.[27] Through therapeutic interventions, we have already mentioned that it is important that mentalization and reflective capacity be promoted, that is, the ability to distance oneself from perceptual immediacy to enter into dialog with one's inner self and in dialog with the other with the world.

Healing according to this view is seen not simply as the resolution of specific symptoms but also as a change in the patient's mode of relating to himself or herself and others.

This may include a greater ability to reflect on one's own experiences, a greater understanding of one's own mental states and those of others, and

[24] For further discussion, see the bibliography: Cozzaglio, P. (2014) Psichiatria intersoggettiva. Dalla cura del soggetto al soggetto della cura. Franco Angeli Publisher, Milan.

[25] For further discussion, see the bibliography: Cozzaglio, P. (2014) Psichiatria intersoggettiva. Dalla cura del soggetto al soggetto della cura. Franco Angeli Publisher, Milan.

[26] For more details, see the bibliography: Carozza P. (2006) Principi di riabilitazione psichiatrica. Per un sistema di servizi orientato alla guarigione. Milano: Franco Angeli.

[27] For more details, see the bibliography: Carozza P. (2006) Principi di riabilitazione psichiatrica. Per un sistema di servizi orientato alla guarigione. Milano: Franco Angeli.

a greater ability to manage interpersonal relationships in a healthier and more constructive way; healing implies a change in the intersubjective field and is to be understood as evolutionary development at the new.[28] This may include a greater ability to reflect on one's own experiences, as mentioned above, a greater understanding of one's own mental states and those of others, and a greater ability to manage interpersonal relationships.[29]

This perspective opposes the view that patients are only mentally ill, classified through diagnostic groupings, labeled as cases for whom the cause of the disease is a chemical imbalance that remains chronic.

According to Cozzaglio,[30] the recovery of reflexivity thus becomes the initial moment of the patient's recovery, but the recovery of reflexivity cannot take place in the complete isolation of the subject, and the social recovery of the subject is also an important condition for the purpose of recovery, as is the development of the reflexive function, which pertains to conscious thinking, not simply that which involves cognitive and conscious functions: reflexive thinking embraces the totality of psychic functions, cognition, affectivity, and feeling.

The subject who develops reflective capacity and the ability to mentalize then comes to a tension of thought similar to what is defined for insight or mindfulness: insight means the ability to see within a situation or within oneself, thus with a perception that is clear, an immediate sharp intuition of external or internal facts, and this generic meaning has acquired specific meanings in psychiatry and psychology to indicate insights and awareness of one's feelings, emotions, and movements of one's behavior; mindfulness, on the other hand, in the field of psychology essentially means awareness of one's thoughts, actions, and motivations; it is a mode of paying moment-to-moment attention to the here and now intentionally to resolve or prevent inner suffering and achieve self-acceptance through greater awareness of one's experience, which includes sensations, perceptions, impulses, emotions, thoughts, words, actions, and relationships.[31]

[28] For further details, see the bibliography: Cozzaglio, P. (2014) Psichiatria intersoggettiva. Dalla cura del soggetto al soggetto della cura. Franco Angeli Publisher, Milan.

[29] For further details, see the bibliography: Cozzaglio, P. (2014) Psichiatria intersoggettiva. Dalla cura del soggetto al soggetto della cura. Franco Angeli Publisher, Milan.

[30] For further details, see the bibliography: Cozzaglio, P. (2014) Psichiatria intersoggettiva. Dalla cura del soggetto al soggetto della cura. Franco Angeli Publisher, Milan.

[31] For further discussion, see the bibliography: Cozzaglio, P. (2014) Psichiatria intersoggettiva. Dalla cura del soggetto al soggetto della cura. Franco Angeli Publisher, Milan.

Facing the Universe After Trauma

Every successful, constructive step toward evolution toward well-being can be metaphorically represented as the abandonment, the death, of a certain stage of evolution to re-emerge at a new level of life, in which the previous stage is not lost but is reworked and summarized at a new evolutionary level—a stage that appears to be the most effective synthesis between the seemingly abandoned and newly established prerogatives.

Irtelli F., 2016, p. 263[32]

Dismantling the whole is the meaninglessness and loneliness and emptiness, the backlash: every successful, constructive step toward an evolution toward well-being can be metaphorically represented as abandonment, or the death of a certain stage of evolution to reemerge at a new level of life, in which the previous stage is not lost but is reworked and summarized at a new evolutionary level, a stage that appears to be the most effective synthesis between the apparently abandoned prerogatives and the newly established ones.[33]

As we have seen in the previous chapters, there are many ways to address trauma and the crisis that may result from the following: in this regard, psychotherapy (which can be of various different orientations), psychopharmacology, or their joint use; in fact, we recall that regarding studies on protocols for dealing with various mental distress, both the effects of psychotropic drugs and the effects of psychotherapy have been studied, and they have shown similar results, and even the dropout rates in the two approaches have been similar (however, we must remember that there can sometimes be side effects regarding drugs),[34] and it is right to recall what we stated earlier: today, we no longer reason according to a logic of opposition between psychotherapy and psychopharmacology, but from the point of view of integration and synergy of both approaches, it will then be the patient with the help of specialists to consciously choose the path best suited to his or her needs, and it must be emphasized that there

[32] For further study, see the bibliography: Irtelli F. (2016) *Illuminarsi di Ben-essere*, Armando, Rome.

[33] For further study, see the bibliography: Irtelli F. (2016) *Illuminarsi di Ben-essere*, Armando, Rome.

[34] For further discussion, see the bibliography: Qaseem A., Barry M.J., Kansagara D. (2016) Nonpharmacologic Versus Pharmacologic Treatment of Adult Patients With Major Depressive Disorder: a Clinical Practice Guideline From the American College of Physicians Ann Intern Med 164 (5): 350–359. doi: https://doi.org/10.7326/MI5-2570.

emerges in every case the need on the part of patients to be able to talk to and be listened to by a professional who can take charge of and understand the problems that are brought, regardless of whether they then prefer a more pharmacological or psychotherapeutic route.[35]

Can one truly be cured through effective treatment?

In this regard, Olsen[36] stated that healing is not going back to old life but is an embrace of a new life with new possibilities. To seek to heal is to aim for the restoration of the condition of belonging to oneself, which drastically contradicts a simple process of making oneself a patient, passively waiting for someone from the outside to dispense for us health and cure for the harm caused by the disease condition.

Healing is first of all rediscovering oneself to think, and we reiterate that healing is not going back to old life; it is an embrace of a new life with new possibilities.[37]

In psychology and psychiatry, therefore, healing is understood as an evolution to the new, evolutionary development to the new, while illness is generally a condition of passivity.[38] We must then remember both that

> *Development is never thought of as an automatic linear becoming.*
> *Tricoli M.L., 2014, p. 12*[39]

[35] For further discussion, see bibliography: Durbano F., Marchesi B., Irtelli F. (2024) Perspective Chapter: Trauma and Depression an Overview about comorbidity In Depression what is new and what is old in human existence, Intehcopen, London; Angermeyer M. C., van der Auwera S., Carta M.G., Schomerus G. (2017) Public attitudes toward Psychiatry and psychiatric treatment at the beginning of the 21st century: a systematic review and meta-analysis of population surveys, World Psychiatry, 16 (1):50–61. doi: https://doi.org/10.1002/wps.20383.

[36] For further discussion, see the bibliography: Olsen E. (2004) *Healing*. Proceedings of the 5th congress of the European Network of ex-users and survivors of psychiatry, Vejle, Denmark, July 17–21, 20 04; Cozzaglio, P. (2014) Psichiatria intersoggettiva. Dalla cura del soggetto al soggetto della cura. Franco Angeli Publisher, Milan.

[37] For further discussion, see the bibliography: Cozzaglio P. (2014) *Intersubjective psychiatry. From the care of the subject to the subject of care*. Franco Angeli, Milan; Olsen E. (2004) Healing. Proceedings of the 5th congress of the European Network of ex-uesers and survivors of psychiatry, Vejle, Denmark, July 17–21, 2004.

[38] For further discussion, see the bibliography: Cozzaglio, P. (2014) Psichiatria intersoggettiva. Dalla cura del soggetto al soggetto della cura. Franco Angeli Publisher, Milan.

[39] For further discussion, see the bibliography: Tricoli M.L. (2014) Preface in Cozzaglio, P. (2014) Psichiatria intersoggettiva. Dalla cura del soggetto al soggetto della cura. Franco Angeli Publisher, Milan.

Both of these essential factors of healing, as anticipated, are the exercise of the reflective function, and we can consider healing as the evolution to the new consistent with the concrete indicators of the exercise of the reflective function, which are the awareness of one's symptoms, the ability to recognize danger and emergency situations, the search for interlocution in one's relationship with one's neighbor, the gaze that goes beyond the limited horizon of one's self and is interested in the world, the capacity for affective resonance in relationships, the search for honest communication with the other, and the search for meaning and significance in what one experiences.[40]

On the other hand, the indicators of new developmental research are activation of desire, activation of the social and affective dimension, activation of the cultural artistic dimension, critical capacity and acceptance of *healthy* dependence on others, ability to maintain gratitude contacts with caregivers, and desire to contribute to social becoming and transformation (such as participation in work or organized social groups and desire to participate in civic life in the social context).[41]

We have described the benefits of therapeutic interventions, and upstream, it is useful to remember that in any course of treatment, regardless of orientation, it is still important to identify and acknowledge the emotions one feels and subsequently accepts them without denying them and wanting to suppress them, place events in space and time because this can help put the traumatic event in perspective, stop seeing change as impossible, and learn to process anger and frustration, which are emotions that are common after trauma (and learning to manage them can be very helpful).

We have dealt in one paragraph with the EMDR technique, but we must remember that there are also many other valid approaches to address mental distress; for example, we can recall that even psychoanalysis is useful in psychotherapy precisely because it promotes the recovery of reflexive function, an important factor in the health of the subject, and recovering one's reflexive function is already a path to healing, and we must remember that there are endless ways that the patient can go in the universe after trauma.

[40] For further discussion, see the bibliography: Cozzaglio, P. (2014) Psichiatria intersoggettiva. Dalla cura del soggetto al soggetto della cura. Franco Angeli Publisher, Milan.

[41] For further discussion, see the bibliography: Cozzaglio, P. (2014) Psichiatria intersoggettiva. Dalla cura del soggetto al soggetto della cura. Franco Angeli Publisher, Milan.

Overall, the patient must play an active role consistent with

> *A vision that aims to emphasize the subject's ability to take charge of his or her own life and direct it to its own shores.*
>
> *It is a matter of liberating human beings from the ancestral propensity to delegation and to envisage the possibility of being creative.*
>
> *Irtelli F., 2016, p. 213*[42]

[42] For further study, see the bibliography: Irtelli F. (2016) *Illuminarsi di Ben-essere*, Armando, Rome.

Appendix

This manuscript proposes contemporary perspectives about trauma and resilience: the book presents an overview of these issues, describing the history of these topics and recent scientific research. Trauma is not always determinative of our life trajectory but depends on our subjective reaction, and recent publications on this topic have analyzed it. The skills underlying resilience can **be strengthened at any age, as it is never too late to build resilience; it is never too late to embark on a path of healing and evolution either.** Resilience is intertwined with the ability to learn, develop relationships with others, motivate oneself to achieve goals, set aspirations and determine how to pursue those goals. All of these aspects can be fostered through **psychotherapy: traumatic** memories are reprocessed in therapy within a safe and empathic space to cope with human life challenges. This book is innovative because it provides an overview of theories that pertain to different fields of psychology: areas pertaining to psychoanalysis, cognitive psychology, EMDR, and many others are explored in depth while also highlighting all the advances that science has made regarding these issues, presenting very recent research. This book can be a valuable contribution to the knowledge of students, mental health professionals, and it can also be a very interesting manuscript for those who want to broaden their knowledge about trauma and resilience. The book is scientific, but it is also very engaging and explains how different perspectives about trauma and resilience can be integrated in light of history and contemporary global scientific research.

© The Author(s), under exclusive license to Springer Nature Switzerland AG 2024
F. Irtelli, F. Gabrielli, *Contemporary Perspectives on Trauma and Resilience*, https://doi.org/10.1007/978-3-031-70793-3

Bibliography

Adler, A. (1927). *Understanding human nature*. Greenberg.

Albasi, C. (2012a). *Attaccamenti traumatici: Modeli operativi interni dissociati*. UTET, Turin University.

Albasi, C. (2012b). *Dissociated Internal Working Models: A relational perspective on attachment, trauma and dissociation*. Nova Science Publishers Inc.

Alder, J., Staldmayr, W., Tschdin, S., & Bitzerb, J. (2006). Posttraumatic symptoms stress after childbirth: What should we offer? *Journal of Psychosomatic Obstetrics & Gynecology, 27*(2), 107–112.

Alvarez-Segura, M., Garcia-Esteve, L., Torres, A., Plaza, A., Imaz, M. L., Hermida-Barros, L., San, L., & Burtchen, N. (2014). Are women with a history of abuse more vulnerable to perinatal depressive symptoms? A systematic review. *Archives of Women's Mental Health, 17*(5), 343–357. https://doi.org/10.1007/s00737-014-0440-9

Amadei, G. (2005). *Come si ammala la mente*. Universale Paperbacks.

American Psychiatric Association, DSM 5 Task Force. (2013). *Diagnostic and statistical manual of mental disorders: DSM-5*™ (5th ed.). American Psychiatric Publishing, Inc., Washington DC, it. Trad. (2014) Raffaello Cortina Editore, Milan.

Ammaniti, M. (1999). *Quei traumi indelebili*. In "La Repubblica" June 2-1999.

Angermeyer, M. C., van der Auwera, S., Carta, M. G., & Schomerus, G. (2017). Public attitudes toward Psychiatry and psychiatric treatment at the beginning of the 21st century: A systematic review and meta-analysis of population surveys. *World Psychiatry, 16*(1), 50–61.

© The Author(s), under exclusive license to Springer Nature Switzerland AG 2024

F. Irtelli, F. Gabrielli, *Contemporary Perspectives on Trauma and Resilience*, https://doi.org/10.1007/978-3-031-70793-3

Anzieu, D. (2012). *Créer-Détruire: Le travail psychique créateur*. Dunod.

Barber, B. A., Kohl, K. L., Kassam-Adams, N., & Gold, J. I. (2014 March). Acute stress, depression, and anxiety symptoms among English and Spanish speaking children with recent trauma exposure. *Journal of Clinical Psychology in Medical Settings, 21*(1), 66–71. https://doi.org/10.1007/s10880-013-9382-z

Barcaccia, B., & Mancini, F. (2013). *Teoria e clinica del perdono*. Raffaello Cortina.

Bauman, Z. (2008). *The art of life*. Polity, Cambridge.

Beck, A. (1976). *Principles of cognitive therapy*. Astrolabe.

Beck, A. T., Rush, A., Shaw, B., & Emery, G. (1979). *Cognitive therapy of depression*. Guilford.

Benson, H., & Allen, R. L. (1980). How much stress is too much. *Harvard Business Review, 58*(5), 86–92.

Berkman, L. F., Glass, T., Brisette, I., & Seeman, T. E. (1979). Social networks, host resistance, and mortality: A nine-year follow-up study of Alameda Country Residents. *American Journal of Epidemiology, 109*, 186–204.

Bertini, M. (2012). *Psicologia della salute*. Raffaello Cortina Publisher.

Biagini, V., Zeonbi, S., Vargas, M., & Marasco, M. (2010). The Stockholm Syndrome: Media phenomenon or psychiatric pathology? *Italian Journal of Criminology, 4*(2), 379–387.

Bleich, A., Kolter, M., & Kultz, I., et al. (2002). *Guidelines for the assessment and professional intervention with terrorist victims in the hospital and the community*. A position paper of the Israeli National Council for Mental Health, Jerusalem, Israel.

Bodenmann, G. (1995). A systemic-transactional conceptualization of stress and coping in couples. *Swiss Journal of Psychology, 54*, 34–49.

Booysen, D. D., & Kagee, D. (2023). Trauma survivors' perceptions and experiences of prolonged exposure for PTSD at a psychology clinic. *South African Journal of Psychiatry*, 1–7. ISSN 2078-6786.

Bowlby, J. (1980). *Attachment and loss, Vol. 3: Loss, sadness and depression*. Hogarth Press and Institute of Psychoanalysis Tr. It. Bollati Boringhieri, Turin, 2001.

Bradley, R., & Greene, J., et al. (2005, February). *A multidimensional meta-analysis of psychotherapy for PTSD* (Vol. 16, pp. 214–277). American Psychiatric Association.

Bromberg, P. M. (2011). *The shadow of the tsunami. The growth of the relational mind*. Tr. it. Raffaello Cortina, Milan, 2012, p. 49.

Burns, D. D. (1980). *Feeling good: The new mood therapy*. Signet.

Butler, J. (2005). *Giving an account of oneself*. Fordham University Press.

Cardinal, M. (2004). *Le parole per dirlo*. Feltrinelli. (Original edition 1975).

Caretti, V., & Capraro, G. (2008). *Trauma e psicopatologia, un approccio evolutivo-relazionale*. Casa Editrice Astrolabio.

Carozza, P. (2006). *Principi di riabilitazione psichiatrica. Per un sistema di servizi orientato alla guarigione*. Franco Angeli.

Certo, S. C. (2003). *Supervision: Concept of skill building* (4th ed.). McGraw Hill.

Ceruti, M. (2018). *Il tempo della Complessità*. Raffaello Cortina Publisher.

Cionini, L. (2013). *Modeli di psicoterapia*. Carocci.

Cohen, S., & Wills, T. A. (1985). Stress, social support, and the buffering hypothesis: A critical review. *Psychological Bulletin, 98*, 310–357.

Combellick, J. L., et al. (2020). Postpartum depression in a cohort of post-9/11 women veterans: The role of military stress and trauma. *Military Behavioral Health*. https://doi.org/10.1080/21635781.2020.1751351

Cordova, M. J., Cunningham, L. L. C., Carlson, C. R., & Andrykowski, M. A. (2001). Posttraumatic growth following breast cancer: A controlled comparison study. *Health Psychology, 20*, 176–185.

Correale, A. (2006). *Area traumatica e campo istituzionale*. Borla Publisher.

Cozzaglio, P. (2014). *Psichiatria intersoggettiva. Dalla cura del soggetto al soggetto della cura*. Franco Angeli Publisher.

Creamer, M., Burgess, P., & McFarlane, A. C. (2001). Posttraumatic stress disorder: Findings from the Australian National Survey of Mental Health and Well-Being. *Psychological Medicine, 31*, 1237–1124.

Cyrulnik, B. (2001). *Les vilains petits canards*. Odile Jacob.

Darley, J. M., & Fazio, R. H. (1980). Expectancy confirmation processes arising in the social interaction sequence. *American Psychologist, 35*, 867–881.

Der Kolk, V., et al. (2007). A Randomized clinical trial of Eye Movement Desensitization and Reprocessing (EMDR), fluoxetine, and pill placebo in the treatment of posttraumatic stress disorder: treatment effects and long-term maintenance. *Journal of Clinical Psychiatry, 68*, 37–46.

Dozois, D. J. A., & Beck, A. T. (2008). Cognitive schemas, beliefs and assumptions. In K. S. Dobson & D. J. A. Dozois (Eds.), *Risk factors in depression* (pp. 121–143). Elsevier/Academic Press.

Durbano, F., Marchesi, B., & Irtelli, F. (2024). Perspective Chapter: Trauma and depression—An overview about comorbidity. In *Depression what is new and what is old in human existence*. IntechOpen.

Dyregrov, A., & Yule, W. (2006). A review of PTSD in children. *Child and Adolescent Mental Health, 11*(4), 176–184. https://doi.org/10.1111/j.1475-3588.2005.00384.x

Easterlin, R. A. (2001). Income and happiness: Toward a unified theory. *The Economic Journal, 111*(473), 465–48412345.

Easterlin, R. A. (2003). Inaugural article: Explaining happiness. *Proceedings of the National Academy of Sciences, 100*(1), 176–183.

Edna, B. F., Keane, T. M., & Friedman, M. (2000). *Effective treatments for PTSD: Practice guidelines from the International Society for Traumatic Stress Studies*. Guilford Press

Eger, E. E. (2021). *Il coraggio di rinascere. Lezioni di resilienza*. Trad. by Lucia Corradini. Corbaccio.

Ehrenberg, A. (2010). *The struggle to be oneself, depression and society*. Einaudi Editore.

Ellis, A. A., Nixon, R. D., & Williamson, P. (2009). The effects of social support and negative appraisals on acute stress symptoms and depression in children and adolescents. *British Journal of Psychology, 48*, 347–361.

Engel, G. L. (1977). The Need for a New Medical Model: A challenge for biomedicine. *Science, 196*, 129–136.

Erickson, M. (1980). *My voice will accompany you*. Astrolabe.

Erickson, M. (1984). *Works volume I–volume IV*. Astrolabe.

Evraire, L. E., & Dozois, D. J. A. (2011). An integrative model of excessive reassurance seeking and negative feedback seeking in the development and maintenance of depression. *Clinical Psychology Review, 31*, 1291–1303.

Fairbairn, R. G. (1952). Endopsychic structures in terms of object-relationships. In *An object relation theory of the personality*. Basic Books.

Fassin, D., & Rechtman, R. (2011). *The empire of trauma, Birth of the victim condition*. Meltemi.

Federici, S. (2017). La rabbia: un'emozione divina, in Paura Rabbia Stupore. Le emozioni e gli altri, Edizione: I, Capitolo 4, Il Margine. Editors: Zoja L., Virgili R., Nori P., Federici S., Petrosino S., Malatesta K., pp. 79–105.

Feldman, R. S., Amoretti, G., & Ciceri, M. R. (2021). *Psicologia generale* (4th ed.). Connect, McGraw Hill Education.

Felitti, V. J., Anda, R. F., Nordenberg, D., Williamson, D. F., Spitz, A. M., Edwards, V., Koss, M. P., & Marks, J. S. (1998). Relationship of childhood abuse and household dysfunction to many of the leading causes of death in adults. The Adverse Childhood Experiences (ACE) Study. *American Journal of Preventive Medicine, 14*, 245–258.

Ferenczi, S. (1932). *Clinical diary. January–October 1932*. Raffaello Cortina, 1988.

Fernandez, I., & Giovannozzi, G. (2012). EMDR and adaptive information processing. Psychotherapy as stimulation of self-repair psychological processes. *Journal of Psychiatry, 47*(1), 1–4.

Fisher, J. (2017). *Guarire la frammentazione del sé. Come integrare le parti del sé dissociate dal trauma psicologico*. Raffaello Cortina Publisher.

Foa, E. B., Johnson, K. M., Feeny, N. C., & Treadwell, K. R. H. (2001). The Child PTSD Symptom Scale: A preliminary examination of its psychometric properties. *Journal of Community Psychology, 30*, 376–384.

Folkman, S. (1997). Positive psychological states and coping with severe stress. *Social Science Medicine, 45*, 1207–1221.

Folkman, S., Lazarus, R. S., Gruen, R. J., & De Longis, A. (1986). Appraisal, coping, health status and psychological symptoms. *Journal of Personality and Social Psychology, 50*(3), 571–579.

Fonagy, P., & Allison, E. (2012). What is mentalization? The concept and its foundations in developmental research and social-cognitive neuroscience. In N. Midgley & I. Vrouva (Eds.), *Minding the child: Mentalization-based interventions with children, young people and their families* (pp. 11–34).

Fonagy, P., & Target, M. (1998). Mentalization and the changing aims of child psychoanalysis. In L. Aron & A. Harris (Eds.), *Relational psychoanalysis: Innovation and expansion* (Vol. 2, pp. 253–278). Analytic Press.

Frances, A. (2013). *Saving normal: An insider's revolt against out-of-control psychiatric diagnosis, DSM-5, big pharma, and the medicalization of ordinary life*. William Morrow & Co.

Frankl, V. E. (1946). *Ein Psychologe erlebt das Konzentrationslager*. Verlag für Jugend und Volk, Vienna, tr. it. Frankl V. E. (2005), *Uno psicologo nei lager*, tr. it. Edizioni Ares, Milan.

Frankl, V. E. (1975). *The unconscious God. Psychotherapy and theology*. Simon & Schuster.

Frankl, V. (1984). *Man's search for meaning*. Simon and Schuster.

Frankl, V. E., & Batthyány, A. (Eds.). (2010). *The feeling of meaninglessness: A challenge to psychotherapy and philosophy* (D. Hallowell, Trans.). Marquette University Press.

Frankl, V. E., Bruzzone, D., & Fizzotti, E. (Eds.). (2005). *La sfida del significato. Analisi esistenziale e ricerca di senso*. Erickson Publisher. TrentoFreud A. (1936) *The ego and the mechanisms of defense* in Works, Vol. 1: Writings 1922–1943, Boringhieri, Turin, 1985.

Freud, F. (1915). *Triebe und Triebschicksale; tradi t Pulsions and their destinies*, in Works, Vol. IX, Turin, Bollati Borighieri, 1986.

Freud, S. (1917). Lutto e melanconia. In *Opere* (Vol. 11). Boringhieri, 1976.

Freud, S. (1920). Jenseits des Lustprinzips. In *Gesammelte Werke* (Vol. 9). The International Psycho-Analytical Press.

Freud, F. (1921). *Jenseits des Lustprinzips*; transl it Beyond the Pleasure Principle, in Works, Vol. IX, Turin, Bollati Borighieri, 1986, p. 215.

Fromm, E. (1971). *The anatomy of human destructiveness*. Holt, Rinehart and Winston.

Fromm, E. (1991). *Die Pathologie der Normalität. Zur Wissenschaft vom Menschen*. Beltz.

Gabrielli, F., & Irtelli, F. (2021). *Introductory Chapter: The transition from distress to acceptance of human frailty—Anthropology and psychology of the pandemic era in anxiety, uncertainty, and resilience during the pandemic period—Anthropological and psychological perspectives*. IntechOpen.

Gladstone, G. L., Parker, G. B., Mitchell, P. B., Malhi, G. S., Wilhelm, et al. (2004). Implications of childhood trauma for depressed women: An analysis of pathways from childhood sexual abuse to deliberate self-harm and revictimization. *American Journal of Psychiatry, 161*, 1417–1425.

Green, B. L. (1994). Traumatic stress and disaster, mental health effects and factors influencing adaptation. In F. Liehmac & C. Nadelson (Eds.), *International Review of Psychiatry* (Vol. 2). American Psychiatric Press.

Hammen, C. L., & Shih, J. (2014). Depression and interpersonal processes. In I. H. Gotlib & C. L. Hammen (Eds.), *Handbook of depression* (pp. 277–295). Guilford.

Harris, M. J., & Rosenthal, R. (1985). Mediation of interpersonal expectancy effect: 31 meta-analyses. *Psychological Bulletin, 97*, 363–386.

Hase, M. (2021). The structure of EMDR therapy: A guide for the therapist. *Frontiers in Psychology, 12.*

Heim, C., Newport, D. J., Mletzko, T., Miller, A. H., & Nemeroff, C. B. (2008). The link between childhood trauma and depression: Insights from HPA axis studies in humans. *Psychoneuroendocrinology, 33*, 693–710.

Herman, J. L. (1992). Complex PTSD: A syndrome in survivors of prolonged and repeated trauma. *Journal of Traumatic Stress, 5*, 377–391.

Horowitz, M. J. (2004). *Sindrome da stress: Valutazione e trattamento.* Raffaello Cortina Publisher.

Horowitz, M., Wilner, N., & Alvarez, W. (1979). Impact of Event Scale: A measure of subjective stress. *Psychosomatic Medicine, 41*, 209–218.

Hughes, S. (1990). Inside madness. *British Medical Journal, 301*, 1476–1478.

Irtelli, F. (2016). *Illuminarsi di Ben-essere.* Armando.

Irtelli, F. (2019). *Rosso smeraldo, l'epoca delle psicosi bianche.* Armando Publisher.

Irtelli, F. (2021). *Sul perdono, l'esperienza umana della rinascita.* La Bussola Publisher.

Irtelli, F., Durbano, F., & Marchesi, B. (2021). The real self and the ideal self. In *Psychoanalysis.* IntechOpen.

Jonas, H. (1984). *The imperative of responsibility: In search of ethics for the technological age* (H. Jonas & D. Herr, Trans.). University of Chicago Press.

Kaptein, A. D., & Weinman, J. (2004). Health psychology: Some introductory remarks. In A. D. Kaptein & J. Weinman (Eds.), *Health psychology.* Blackwell Publishing.

Kendler, K. S., Kuhn, J. W., & Prescott, C. A. (2004). Childhood sexual abuse, stressful life events and risk for major depression in women. *Psychological Medicine, 34*, 1475–1482.

Kernberg, O. (2014). Preface in Mucci C. *Trauma e perdono*, una prospettiva intergenerazionale. Raffaello Cortina Publisher.

Lazarus, R. S. (1966). *Psychological stress and the coping process.* McGraw-Hill.

Lazarus, R. S. (1993). *Coping theory and research: Past, present and future. Psychosomatic medicine.* American Psychosomatic Society.

Lazarus, R. S., & Folkman, S. (1984). *Stress, appraisal and coping.* Springer.

Lee, K. A., et al. (1995). A 50-year prospective study of the psychological sequelae of World War Combat. *American Journal of Psychiatry, 152*, 516–522.

Levinas, E. (1969). *Totality and infinity: An essay on exteriority* (A. Lingis, Trans.). Duquesne University Press.

Lingiardi, V. (2014). Preface in Mucci C. *Trauma e perdono, una prospettiva psicoanalitica intergenerazionale*. Raffaello Cortina Publisher.

Liotti, G. (2005). Trauma and dissociation in the light of attachment theory. *Childhood and Adolescence, 4*(3), 130–144.

Lowen, A. (1972). *La depressione e il corpo. La base biologica della fede e della realtà*. Astrolabio Ubaldini Publisher.

Matthijssen, S. J. M. A., et al. (2020). The current status of EMDR therapy, specific target areas, and goals for the future. *Journal of EMDR Practice and Research, 14*(4), 241–284.

McWilliams, N. (1999). *La diagnosi psicoanalitica*. Astrolabio Publisher.

Meichenbaum, D. (1994). *A clinical handbook/Practical therapist manual for assessing and treating adults with Post Traumatic Stress Disorder (PTSD)*. Institute Press, University of Waterloo.

Mellman, T. A., et al. (1992). Phenomenology and runs of psychiatric disorders associated with combat-related posttraumatic stress disorder. *American Journal of Psychiatry, 149*, 1568–1574.

Merton, R. (1948). The self-fulfilling prophecy. *Antioch Review, 8*, 193–210.

Miller, E. (1940). *Neuroses in war*. Macmillan.

Mucci, C. (2014). *Trauma e perdono, una prospettiva intergenerazionale*. Raffaello Cortina Publisher.

Nelson, E. C., Heath, A. C., Madden, P. A., Cooper, M. L., Dinwiddie, S. H., Bucholz, K. K., Glowinski, A., McLaughlin, T., Dunne, M. P., Statham, D. J., & Martin, N. G. (2002). Association between self-reported childhood sexual abuse and adverse psychosocial outcomes: Results from a twin study. *Archives of General Psychiatry, 59*, 139–145.

Nussbaum, M. C. (1986). *The fragility of goodness: Luck and ethics in Greek tragedy and philosophy*. Cambridge University Press.

O'Donnell, M. L., Creamer, M., & Pattison, P. (2004). Posttraumatic stress disorder and depression following trauma: Understanding comorbidity. *American Journal of Psychiatry, 161*, 1390–1396.

Olsen, E. (2004). *Healing*. In Proceedings of the 5th congress of the European Network of ex-users and survivors of psychiatry, Vejle, Denmark, July 17–21, 2004.

Oquendo, M. A., Friend, J. M., Batsheva Halberstam, B. A., & Brodsky, B. S. (2003, March). Association of comorbid posttraumatic stress disorder and major depression with greater risk for suicidal behavior. *American Journal of Psychiatry, 160*, 580–582.

Penk, W. E. (1989). Posttraumatic stress disorder: Selected issues. *Journal of Clinical Psychology, XLV*(5), 688–832.

Pierce, Z. P., Johnson, E. R., et al. (2023). Therapeutic interventions impact brain function and promote posttraumatic growth in adults living with posttraumatic stress disorder: A systematic review and meta-analysis of functional magnetic resonance imaging studies. *Frontiers in Psychology, 14.*

Qaseem, A., Barry, M. J., & Kansagara, D. (2016). Nonpharmacologic versus pharmacologic treatment of adult patients with major depressive disorder: A clinical practice guideline from the American College of Physicians. *Annals of Internal Medicine, 164*(5), 350–359.

Rogers, C. R. (1942). *Counseling and psychotherapy: Newer concepts in practice.* Houghton Mifflin.

Rogers, C. (1951). *Client-centered therapy: Its current practice, implications and theory.* La Meridiana.

Rogers, C. (1961). *On becoming a person.* Little, Brown Book Group.

Ryul, J., Kim, Y., Yun, H., Han, D., & Choi, N. (2016). Trauma, depression, and resilience among women living with HIV/AIDS in Kenya. *International Journal of Psychology and Behavioral Sciences, 6*(2), 76–81. https://doi.org/10.5923/j.ijpbs.20160602.07

Salmon, K., & Bryant, R. A. (2002). Posttraumatic stress disorder in children: The influence of developmental factors. *Clinical Psychological Review, 22*, 163–188.

Salvo, A. (1994). *Depressione e sentimenti, l'incapacità di essere felici.* Mondadori Publisher.

Scelles, C., Bulnes, L. C., et al. (2021). EMDR as treatment option for conditions other than PTSD: A systematic review. *Frontiers in Psychology, 12.*

Schwaryz, H. L. (1994). From dissociation to negotiation: A relational psychoanalytic perspective on multiple personality disorder. *Psychoanalytic Psychology, 11*, 189–231.

Seligman, M. E. P. (1977). *Helplessness: On depression, development and death.* Freeman.

Selye, H. (1936). A syndrome produced by different nocuous agents. *Nature, 138*, 32.

Selye, H. (1964). *From dream to discovery.* McGraw Hill.

Selye, H. (1993). History of the stress concept. In *Handbook of stress: Theoretical and clinical aspects.*

Seyle, H. (1987). *Stress without distress.* Transword.

Sgarro, M. (1998). *Post traumatic stress disorder, aspetti clinici e psicoterapie.* Kappa.

Shapiro, F. (1989). Eye Movement Desensitization: A new treatment for posttraumatic stress disorder. *Journal of Behavior Therapy and Experimental Psychiatry, 20*, 211–217.

Shapiro, F. (1995). *Eye Movement Desensitization and Reprocessing (EMDR): Basic principles, protocols, and procedures.* Guilford Press.

Shapiro, F. (1999). Eye Movement Desensitization and Reprocessing (EMDR) and the anxiety disorder: Clinical and research implications of an integrated psychotherapy treatment. *Journal of Anxiety Disorders, 13*, 35–67.

Shonkoff, J. P., Levitt, P., Bunge, S., et al. (2015). *Supportive relationships and active skill-building strengthen the foundations of resilience*. Working Paper No. 13. National Scientific Council on the Developing Child, Harvard University.

Siegel, D. (2012). *The developing mind: How relationships an d the brain interact to shape who we are*. Guilford Press.

Smith, E. R., & Mackie, D. M. (2004). *Social psychology*. Zanichelli.

Spanocchi, P., & Cenerini, M. (2001). *Stress, trauma and psychotherapy in everyday emergencies*. Medicea.

St. Aubyn, E. (1992). *The Melrose*. Tr. it. Neri Pozza, Vicenza 2012.

Stoia-Caraballo, R., et al. (2008). Negative affect and anger rumination as mediators between forgiveness and sleep quality. *Journal of Behavioral Medicine, 31*(6), 478–488.

Sutker, P. B., Uddo-Crane, M., & Allain, A. (1991). Clinical and research assessment of posttraumatic stress disorder: A conceptual overview. *A Journal of Consulting and Clinical Psychology, 3*(4), 520–530.

Tedeschi, R. G., & Calhoun, L. G. (1996). The posttraumatic growth inventory: Measuring the positive legacy of trauma. *Journal of Traumatic Stress, 9*, 455–471.

Tedeschi, R. G., & Calhoun, L. G. (2004). Posttraumatic growth: Conceptual foundations and empirical evidence. *Psychological Inquiry, 15*, 1–18.

Tedeschi, R. G., Park, C. L., & Calhoun, L. G. (1998). Posttraumatic growth; Conceptual issues. In R. G. Tedeschi, C. L. Park, & L. G. Calhoun (Eds.), *Posttraumatic growth: Positive changes in the aftermath of crisis* (pp. 1 22). Lawrence Erlbaum Associates, Publishers.

Terr, L. C. (1979). Children of Chowchilla. A study of psychic terror. *The Psychoanalytic Study of the Child, 34*, 547–623.

Terr, L. C. (1983). Chowchilla revisited: The effect of psychic trauma four years after a school-bus kidnapping. *American Journal of Psychiatry, 140*, 1543–1550.

Terr, L. (1994). *Unchained memories. True stories of traumatic memories, lost and found*. Basic Books.

Tricoli, M. L. (2014). Preface in Cozzaglio, P. *Psichiatria intersoggettiva. Dalla cura del soggetto al soggetto della cura*. Franco Angeli Publisher.

Tronick, E. (2022). Trauma never occurs only once: Being traumatized by a slap is like making meaning of the game of peek-a-boo. *Psychoanalytic Dialogs, 32*(6), 661–673.

Trunzo, J. J., & Pinto, B. M. (2003). Social support as a mediator of optimism and distress in breast cancer survivors. *Journal of Consulting and Clinical Psychology, 71*, 805–811.

Tummala-Narra, P. (2023). Awakening to racial trauma faced by Asian Americans. *Psychoanalytic Dialogs, 33*(1), 77–86.

Uchino, B. N. (2004). *Social support and physical health: Understanding the health consequences of relationships.* Yale University Press.

Uchino, B. N. (2006). Social support and health: A review of psychological processes potentially underlying links to disease outcomes. *Journal of Behavioral Medicine, 29*(4), 377–386.

Uchino, B. N., Cacioppo, J. T., & Kiecolt-Glaser, J. K. (1996). The relationship between social support and psychological processes: A review with emphasis on underlying mechanisms and implications for health. *Psychological Bulletin, 119*, 488–531.

Uchino, B. N., Bowen, K., Kent de Gray, R., Mikel, J., & Fisher, E. B. (2018). Social support and physical health: Models, mechanisms, and opportunities. In *Principles and concepts of behavioral medicine.* Springer.

van der Kolk, B. (2003). The neurobiology of childhood trauma and abuse. *Child and Adolescent Psychiatric Clinics of North America, 12*, 293–317.

Vergani, M. (2015). *Responsibility. Responding to the self, responding to the other.* Raffaello Cortina.

Wiesel, E. (1997). *Ethics and memory. Ethic und Erinnerung.* Walter de Gruyter.

Williams, R. (Ed.). (2009). *Trauma e relazioni, le prospettive scientifiche e cliniche contemporanee.* Raffaello Cortina Publisher.

Wilson, J. P., & Keane, T. M. (1997). *Assessing psychological trauma and PTSD.* Guilford Press.

World Health Organization (1948) Constitution of the World Health organization, .

Yan, S., Shan, Y., Zhong, S., Miao, H., Luo, Y., Ran, H., & Jia, Y. (2021). The effectiveness of eye movement desensitization and reprocessing toward adults with major depressive disorder: A meta-analysis of randomized controlled trials. *Frontiers in Psychiatry, 12.*

Yao, S. N., Cottraux, J., De Mey-Guillard, C., Mollard, E., & Ventureyra, V. (2003, May–June). Evaluation of posttraumatic stress disorder: Validation of a measure, the PCLS. *Encephale, 29*(3pt), 232–238.

Yerkes, R. M., & Dodson, J. D. (1908). The relation of strength of stimulus to rapidity of habit-formation. *Journal of Comparative Neurology and Psychology, 18*, 459–482.

Yule, W. (1997). *Anxiety, depression and posttraumatic stress in childhood. Child Psychology Portfolio.* NFER-NELSON.

Yule, W. (2000). *Post-traumatic stress disorder, aspetti clinici e terapia.* McGraw-Hill.

Yule, W., Perrin, S., & Smith, P. (1999). Posttraumatic stress reactions in children and adolescents. In W. Yule (Ed.), *Posttraumatic stress disorders: Concepts and therapy.* Wiley.

Yunitri, N., Kao, C. C., Chu, H., Voss, J., Chiu, H. L., Liu, D., Shen, S. T. H., Chang, P. C., Kang, X. L., & Chou, K. R. (2020). The effectiveness of eye movement desensitization and reprocessing toward anxiety disorder: A meta-analysis of randomized controlled trials. *Journal of Psychiatric Research, 123*, 102–113.

Zacchetti, E., & Castelnuovo, G. (2021). *Il trattamento della depressione tra illusioni e speranze, esperienze e interventi in psicologia clinica*. Franco Angeli Publisher.

Index[1]

[1] Note: Page numbers followed by 'n' refer to notes.

© The Author(s), under exclusive license to Springer Nature Switzerland AG 2024

F. Irtelli, F. Gabrielli, *Contemporary Perspectives on Trauma and Resilience*, https://doi.org/10.1007/978-3-031-70793-3

SPRINGER NATURE

GPSR Compliance

The European Union's (EU) General Product Safety Regulation (GPSR) is a set of rules that requires consumer products to be safe and our obligations to ensure this.

If you have any concerns about our products, you can contact us on ProductSafety@springernature.com

In case Publisher is established outside the EU, the EU authorized representative is:

Springer Nature Customer Service Center GmbH
Europaplatz 3
69115 Heidelberg, Germany

The manufacturer's authorised representative in the EU is Springer Nature Customer Service Centre GmbH, Europaplatz 3, 69115 Heidelberg, Germany. If you have any concerns regarding our products, please contact ProductSafety@springernature.com

Printed and bound by CPI Group (UK) Ltd, Croydon, CR0 4YY
30/09/2026
02225609-0006